COMPLETE ELECTRIC SMKER COOKBOOK

FOR EFFORTLESS SMOKING

Simple & Juicy Smoker Recipes
To Lick Your Fingers

JOHN SNIDER

CONTENTS

Vegetables, Snacks, and Sides..98

INTRODUCTION

Hello, smoker! Thanks for purchasing my cookbook - I hope you're enjoying your electric smoker. It's more than a kitchen appliance. It's an opportunity to enjoy the sun, share a great time with friends and family, and talk and laugh while enjoying tasty smoking food.

Smoking is the process of using heat to infuse food with a smoky flavor. Smoking blends a heat source with some fragrant wood to infuse flavor into food. Smoking enthusiasts typically smoke big hunks of meat like brisket or lots of racks of ribs. This can take hours, depending on the size of the meat.

If you're a fan of smoked food, you've probably been tempted to try smoking some yourself. But if you've never done it before, the process can seem intimidating—and that's where I come in!

I'm going to take you through the basics of smoking food with a smoker so that whether you're after turkey or pork belly, we'll have all the information you need to get started.

I love to cook, so I'm so excited to share my favorite recipes with you! I've put all my experience into this book, so it'll show you the best recipes with easy-to-follow directions, spices, sauces and cuts so that your dishes are unforgettable. With these home cooking recipes, you will enjoy eating like never before.

Many of the recipes in this book are for large cuts of meat like pulled pork, rack of lamb, whole chicken, ribs, vegetables, and more. But anything you can cook in the oven, you can grill on the Electric Smoker - adding more flavor with this fantastic kiss of wood-fired smoke.

Although there are many brands and different models of electric smokers, the recipes in this book are ready to be prepared with just any model out there. Also, feel free to make little adjustments based on your own taste, preference or fantasy! You can adjust cooking temperate or time without worrying that it's not exactly the way this book tells you it should be. Let's smoke!

How to Start Using an Electric Smoker

A smoker is a device that cooks food in a low, smoky environment. It's an ideal way to prepare meat, poultry, seafood, and vegetables at home — with the added bonus of being able to use your own wood chips for flavoring!

The first step is to prep your smoker by preheating it to 250-300 degrees Fahrenheit or (120-150 degrees Celcius). This will help season the unit's interior and prevent any rust from developing.

Next, add some wood chips to your smoker and light them up. You'll want to allow them to burn for about 10 minutes before adding your meat or fish. Add water to the water pan if desired. The water will keep your meat moist and flavorful as it cooks. It also adds moisture to your smoking, which helps prevent a dry, harsh result.

Then, add food, ensuring that it's on a rack so that air can circulate around it and keep it from getting too charred on one side. You should also use tongs to turn the meat regularly while cooking so that all sides get exposed evenly.

Smoke for 2 hours or until the meat is done, checking every hour to refill wood chips if necessary.

Finally, make sure there are no loose wires anywhere inside or outside your smoker! Loose wires create sparks, which could cause an emergency situation if left unchecked during use.

A Simple Guide to Enjoy Smoking Food

1. Start with a good recipe and seasoning - you have the best options in this book.

2. Select your wood. Experiment with your tastes and find what works best for you.

   - **Apple** is sweet and mild and offers a mild smoke flavor. It's great for fish, poultry, and other meats like pork chops and chicken breasts.

   - **Cherry** gives the meat a sweet flavor that goes well with game birds like duck or pheasant. It also goes well with pork and salmon.

   - **Hickory** has a robust and rich taste that complements beef very well. It's also great with lamb and pork ribs.

- **Maple** is mellow and sweet—it's perfect for fish or poultry because it doesn't overpower them. You can also use it on vegetables like squash or carrots if you want a subtle sweetness in addition to their natural flavors.

- **Mesquite** has a bold flavor that works well on meaty foods like ribs or steak (if you're looking for something with more kick). It's also good on poultry such as chicken wings or legs because the flavor is bold enough not to get lost in all those other flavors!

- **Peach** is fruity without being overwhelming — it works well on poultry or pork, but it can also be used for beef if you want something a little sweeter than hickory or mesquite.

- **Pecan** is a flavored nut that pairs well with fish and shellfish.

- **Walnut** has a sweet, slightly bitter flavor that goes well with beef and pork. It also works great with poultry.

3. Make sure your smoker is clean before each use.

4. Prep your smoker. It's recommended preheating it for at least 30 minutes before you start cooking, so it's nice and hot when you put your meat in there. This will also make sure that all of the juices stay in place as they cook instead of dripping onto the coals below (which is what happens if you don't preheat).

5. Don't put too much wood in your smoker. Use dry wood and soak it for at least 24 hours before smoking.

6. Keep an eye on the temperature! Ensure the temperature is between 225-300 degrees Fahrenheit (120-150 degrees Celcius) for best results.

7. Use a thermometer. It's best to use an accurate thermometer to monitor your meat's internal temperature and ensure it never gets above 165°F (75°C). That way you'll avoid overcooking your food and having a challenging, dry piece of meat on your hands!

8. Use fresh ingredients. Fresh ingredients are essential to an excellent smokehouse flavor. The difference between using fresh ingredients and frozen ones is enormous! Fresh veggies, meat, and fruit will give you the best results when creating delicious smoked foods.

9. Let your meat sit loosely covered with foil before slicing for a few minutes. This will give the juices a chance to settle and stay in the meat, which will make it juicier and more tender.

10. Serve and enjoy the smoking food!

Which is The Best Meat to Smoke?

Surely you have wondered more than once what is the best meat to smoke. Although this method of cooking meats results in delicious and pleasing flavors for our palates, not all meats are as rich, tasty, and juicy as those prepared this way.

Beef

Beef has a flavor that makes it great for smoking. Thanks to its juiciness, intensity of flavor and versatility of cuts, it is one of the meats that most people like to eat. The most popular cuts are beef brisket and beef ribs. However, the steak, beef cheek, chuck roast, prime beef rib, tri-tip and sirloin also give outstanding results.

Pork

Pork is another excellent option for smoking meats because it is cheap and delicious. There are a variety of cuts to choose from that are really rich: shoulder, ribs, sausage, pork belly or bacon. If you want the best result, avoid less thin pieces, such as chops or tenderloin, because they are less juicy.

Chichen

Chicken is another great choice. It cooks quickly, is tender and more digestible than other types of meat. It is also a healthy option for those who are careful about their diet. Spatchcock chicken, wings, thighs, and drumsticks are great choices because they have a lot of flavor and texture.

Lamb

Lamb has a rich flavor that goes well with many different sauces. For a maximum taste, opt for the leg or shoulder. These are the fattiest parts and will guarantee that they are delicious.

The Best Vegetables to Smoke

Smoking vegetables is one of the most classic traditions of preparing smoking dishes. So, which are the best ones to smoke?

First and foremost, you need to pick a good vegetable. While all vegetables can be smoked, there are some better than others. Here's my list of recommendations:

Asparagus

Asparagus is one of the most popular smoked vegetables—for a good reason! It's easy to prepare and delicious when finished. You'll want to trim off the bottom inch or so of each spear so that it sits flat in your smoker rack.

Eggplant

Eggplant works well as a side dish or an appetizer served with dip or sauce. You'll want to cut your eggplant into long strips about 1/4" thick before smoking them so that they cook evenly throughout (you can also try slicing them lengthwise into strips)

Green beans

Green beans are another common choice for smokers—they're easy to prepare and tasty when finished! Trim off the stems from your green beans. Then lay them out flat on an aluminum foil-lined baking sheet before placing them in your smoker at a temperature of 250°F with smoke flowing freely through until they're tender.

Carrots

Carrots are sweet and rich in beta-carotene, which gives them their bright orange color. They're also rich in vitamin A, which is good for your eyesight and immune system. It would be a good idea to slice it or cut it in half. Although if you put it on a skewer, along with other vegetables, you will get a better result when smoking them.

Bell Peppers

Smoked bell peppers is a great way to add a smokey flavor to your dishes. They are high in vitamin C, which can help fight off colds and other illnesses.

Tips for Playful and Rich Smoking Food

Are you new to smoking? Or maybe you've been enjoying it for some time, but you're looking to improve your game. Well, there's an easy solution. It's an electric smoker. I will give you a series of tips to help you make the best smoking food in your neighborhood.

Most important of all, think about what you want to cook. Depending on the type of food, the process may take longer or shorter than others.

The first option is **the meat**. The smell and taste of smoked meat are irresistible. The best food to smoke is all the meats. From steaks, pork, and chicken to lamb, sausages, and even side dishes, you can smoke anything and be pleased with the results.

Fish for a healthy diet. Smoking fish is a nice way to preserve and give it a delicious flavor. You can smoke fish such as sardines, tuna, salmon, monkish or sea bream... And you shouldn't forget about seafood, barbecued delicious prawns, crabs, mussels, clams... even squid and cuttlefish can be smoked!

Other foods.

- The **vegetables** are indispensable as an accompaniment to fish and meat.

- Although it may seem strange, **fruits** can also be smoked, such as pears, pineapples or bananas. effortless, and they get a sugary taste. They are usually prepared on skewers as desserts or used to flavor meats.

- **Cheese** is another protagonist of the smoking. It can be smoked a little so that it melts a little, and you can use it on any meat.

About the recipes

You're going to love this cookbook. It's full of recipes that are easy to follow and prepare, with so many delicious flavors you can't help but try them all. You'll find that the recipes have been selected to teach techniques specific to electric smoking, so you can master this new skill with ease.

With each recipe you make, you'll learn a new technique or two, and before long you'll be able to source ingredients with ease. Many of the meat cuts are very affordable and they taste amazing when prepared correctly and smoked at low and slow temperatures. This cookbook is full of those tips, which will limit frustration and help you fall in love with smoking!

NOTE!

The recipes in this cookbook give estimated preparation and cook times for your convenience. The actual time may vary based on the model of your electric smoker.

BEEF AND LAMB RECIPES

Flavorful Beef Burnt Ends with Mop Sauce

Prep Time: 40 minutes + marinating time | Cook Time: 7 hours | Serves 8

Ingredients

3 tbsp paprika

2 cups packed dark brown sugar

3 tbsp chili powder

3 tbsp lemon pepper

Salt and ground black pepper to taste

3 tbsp garlic powder

3 tbsp onion powder

1 tsp mustard powder

4 lb beef brisket point cut, trimmed

Mop Sauce

½ cup packed dark brown sugar

1 cup apple cider vinegar

½ cup treacle

½ cup brandy

2 chopped canned chipotle peppers in adobo sauce

3 tbsp Worcestershire sauce

3 tbsp tomato purée

3 tbsp garlic powder

3 tbsp onion powder

1 tbsp fine sea salt

1 lemon, juiced

Directions

Pour the mop sauce ingredients into a large jar and shake them to combine well. Seal with lid and set aside until ready to use. Blend the paprika, sugar, chili powder, lemon pepper, black pepper, garlic powder, onion powder, mustard powder, and salt in a bowl.

Apply the rub evenly over the brisket and wrap it tightly in cling film. Marinate in the refrigerator the brisket for 12-24 hours.

Preheat your electric smoker to 225°F by adding mild or wood chips. Take out the beef from the refrigerator and remove the cling film. Preheat a large cast-iron skillet on a smoking rack.

Add the brisket to a smoking rack and smoke for 5-6 hours until tender. Remove the brisket from the heat to a cutting board and leave it to cool, loosely covered with foil.

Then, cut the brisket into cubes and transfer them to the preheated cast-iron skillet. Pour in half of the mop sauce and toss to coat. Put back the skillet in the smoker and cook for 20-30 minutes, tossing the meat often. Spoon the remaining mop sauce over the meat and serve.

Fiesta Peppercorn-Crusted Beef Tenderloin

Prep Time: 45 minutes | Cook Time: about 2 hours | Serves 6

Ingredients

2 tbsp unsalted butter

2 tbsp olive oil

1 center-cut beef tenderloin

1 cup black peppercorns, partially crushed

¼ tsp crushed red pepper flakes

1 yellow onion, finely diced

3 garlic cloves, crushed

2 tbsp chopped thyme

Salt and ground black pepper to taste

1 cup bourbon

1 cup heavy cream

1 tbsp mixed peppercorns, crushed

Directions

Preheat your electric smoker to 275°F by adding apple wood chips. Preheat a large cast-iron skillet on a smoking rack and add the butter. Drizzle the beef with olive oil, then roll it in the crushed black peppercorns to coat.

To the preheated skillet, add the yellow onion, garlic, thyme, red pepper flakes, salt, and pepper and stir. Put the beef on the smoking rack above the skillet and smoke for 55-60 minutes. Pour the bourbon into the skillet to deglaze it, scraping up any brown bits from the bottom.

Pour in the heavy cream and mixed peppercorns and continue smoking the beef until the internal temperature reaches 150°F for medium-well and 160°F for well-done. Remove the beef to a cutting board and leave it to rest, loosely covered with foil, for 15-20minutes. Spoon the cooking juices over the meat and serve.

Chili BBQ Baby Back Ribs

Prep Time: 40 minutes | Cooking Time: 6 hours | Serves: 6

Ingredients

2 tsp salt

4 lb slabs baby back ribs

1 tsp chili powder

½ tsp garlic pepper

1 tsp paprika

1 tsp black pepper

2 tsp lemon juice

2 tsp BBQ sauce

Directions

Cut the baby back ribs into pieces. Mix the remaining ingredients in a bowl. Rub the mixture on the baby back ribs. Put the baby back ribs in the electric smoker at 225°F for 6 hours.

Parmesan Beef Meatballs

Prep Time: 45 minutes | Cook Time: about 2 hours | Serves 8

Ingredients

2 tbsp olive oil
2 yellow onions, cut into rings
3 lb ground beef
8 bacon slices, chopped
2 tbsp fresh oregano, chopped
2 large eggs, lightly beaten
1 tbsp Worchestershire sauce

1 tsp chili powder
1 cup fresh bread crumbs
Salt and ground black pepper to taste
4 cups tomato sauce
4 cups beef stock
2 cups red wine
3 oz grated Parmesan cheese

Directions

Preheat your electric smoker to 225°F by adding hickory smoker chips. Preheat a large cast-iron casserole on a smoking rack and add the olive oil and yellow onion rings.

Place the ground beef, bacon, oregano, eggs, Worchestershire sauce, salt, pepper, chili powder, and bread crumbs in a large bowl and mix the ingredients together thoroughly with your hands. Shape the meat mixture into balls and arrange them on smoking racks above the casserole.

Pour the tomato sauce, beef stock, and red wine into the casserole and stir to combine. Smoke the meatballs for 55-60 minutes, then add them to the casserole. Continue smoking for 50-60 minutes or until the internal temperature reaches 160°F. Scatter with Parmesan and serve.

Easy Beef Tri-Tip

Prep Time: 40 minutes + marinating time | Cook Time: 3 hours | Serves 6

Ingredients

½ cup coarse sea salt
½ cup packed light brown sugar
1 tbsp peppercorns, whole
1 tsp allspice berries, whole
1 chili pepper, sliced
½ tsp cloves, whole
3 fresh bay leaves

2 cups ice water
½ tsp garlic powder
1 tsp onion powder
1 (4-lb) tri-tip beef roast, trimmed
2 tsp olive oil
Salt and ground black pepper to taste

Directions

Place a saucepan over medium heat. Add the sugar, peppercorns, allspice, cloves, bay leaves, chili, salt, and pepper. Stir until the sugar is dissolved, then remove from the heat. Pour in the ice water to cool the marinade. Add the beef and cover it with plastic wrap. Marinate in the refrigerator for 12 hours, turning twice.

Preheat your electric smoker to 225°F by adding hickory smoker chips. Remove the beef and pat it dry with kitchen towels. Discard the brine. Drizzle the tri-tip with olive oil and sprinkle it with garlic powder, onion powder, salt, and pepper on all sides.

Put the meat on a smoking tray. Smoke for 2-3 hours or until the internal thermometer reads 125°F for rare, 135°F for medium-rare, and 160°F for well-done. Remove the beef from the heat and let it rest covered with foil for 15-20 minutes. Serve warm.

Cheese & Red Onion Hamburgers

Prep Time: 45 minutes | Cook Time: about 1 hour | Serves 4

Ingredients

2 tbsp olive oil

2 tbsp unsalted butter

2 red onions, cut into ½-inch rings

2 thyme sprigs, finely chopped

Salt and ground black pepper to taste

2 lb ground beef

8 smoked bacon slices

1 lb aged Monterey Jack cheese, shredded

4 burger buns

4 tomatoes, sliced

2 Dill pickles, thinly sliced lengthwise

Directions

Preheat your electric smoker to 250°F by adding hickory smoker chips. Preheat a large cast-iron casserole on a smoking rack and pour in the olive oil and butter.

Add the red onions, thyme, salt, and pepper and stir to combine. Smoke for 8-10 minutes or until onions are tender. Take out the skillet from the heat and set it aside.

Season the ground beef with salt and pepper and shape it into 4 balls; flatten to make 4 hamburgers. Cover them with bacon and transfer them to smoking racks. Smoke for 50-60 minutes or until thoroughly cooked.

Top the burger with shredded Monterey Jack cheese and continue smoking for 8-10 minutes until the cheese is melted. Add the cheeseburgers to the burger buns and top with tomatoes and pickles to serve.

American-Style Osso Buco

Prep Time: 40 minutes | Cook Time: 3 hours |Serves 4

Ingredients

4 tbsp canola oil

2 tbsp unsalted butter

4 bone-in beef shanks, tied with butcher's twine

Salt and ground black pepper to taste

2 cups diced carrots

2 cups diced celery

2 cups diced sweet onions

4 garlic cloves, minced

2 tsp Italian seasoning

3 fresh bay leaves

3 tbsp passata

½ cup all-purpose flour

3 cups dry white wine

3 cups vegetable broth

2 lemons, zested

2 lemons, cut into slices

Directions

Preheat your electric smoker to 250°F by adding apple wood chips. Preheat a cast-iron casserole on a smoking rack and add the canola oil. Sprinkle the beef shanks with salt and pepper.

To the preheated casserole, add the carrots, celery, onions, garlic, Italian seasoning, bay leaves, salt, and pepper and stir. Smoke for 60 minutes. Put the beef on the smoking rack above the skillet and smoke for 55-60 minutes.

Stir the passata and flour in a bowl and add the mixture into the casserole. Deglaze the casserole by adding dry white wine; scrape up any browned bits from the bottom with a wooden spatula.

Pour in the vegetable broth and add the beef shanks. Continue smoking for another 60 minutes until you reach the desired texture, spooning the cooking sauce over the shanks frequently. Discard the bay leaves and sprinkle with lemon zest. Serve with lemon slices.

Sirloin Steak with Chimichurri & Pine Nuts

Prep Time: 40 minutes | Cook Time: about 1 hour | Serves 4

Ingredients

1 lime, zested and juiced

1 bunch of fresh parsley, chopped

2 garlic cloves, minced

1 cup extra-virgin olive oil

1 tsp red wine vinegar

½ tsp chili powder

Salt and ground black pepper to taste

4 beef sirloin steaks

3 tbsp pine nuts

Directions

Put the lime juice, zest, parsley, garlic, olive oil, vinegar, chili powder, salt, and pepper in a mixing bowl and stir with a whisk to combine. Let the resulting chimichurri sit for 5-10 minutes to release all of the flavors into the oil before using.

Preheat your electric smoker to 275°F and add cherry wood chips. Salt and pepper the beef on both sides. Spread half of the chimichurri sauce over the meat with your hands.

Smoke the meat for 55-60 minutes or until the internal thermometer reads 125°F for rare, 135°F for medium-rare, and 160°F for well-done.

Remove the steaks from the heat to a cutting board and cover them with foil to rest for 5-10 minutes. Cut the meat into thin slices and arrange them on a platter. Garnish with pine nuts and serve with the remaining chimichurri sauce.

Au Jus Beef Shank Roast

Prep Time: 40 minutes | Cook Time: 4 hours | Serves 4

Ingredients

Salt and ground black pepper to taste
1 (5-lb) bone-in beef shank roast
2 tbsp olive oil
1 carrot, chopped
12 shiitake mushrooms, quartered
12 garlic cloves, halved lengthwise

8 shallots, halved lengthwise
3 thyme sprigs
3 cups white wine
2 fresh bay leaves
4 cups beef stock

Directions

Preheat your electric smoker to 225°F by adding hickory smoker chips. Salt and pepper the beef shank roast. Preheat a large cast-iron skillet on a smoking rack and pour in the olive oil. Add the carrot, mushrooms, garlic, shallots, thyme, salt, and pepper and stir to combine.

Smoke for 10-15 minutes until tender. Deglaze the skillet with wine, scraping up any brown bits from the bottom. Pour in the stock and bay leaves and insert the skillet into the smoker.

Put the beef on a smoking rack directly above the skillet and smoke for 50-60 minutes. Then move the roast to the skillet with vegetables, pouring the cooking juices over it.

Continue smoking until the internal thermometer reaches 160°F for well-done. Slide out the skillet and let it rest covered with foil for 10-15 minutes. Remove and discard the bay leaves and thyme. Slice and serve with the mushrooms, garlic, and shallots, topped with au jus.

Pancetta-Wrapped Meatloaf

Prep Time: 45 minutes | Cook Time: about 2 hours | Serves 8

Ingredients

2 tbsp olive oil

1 yellow onion, finely diced

4 garlic cloves, minced

1 tbsp fresh thyme, chopped

½ tsp mustard powder

½ porcini powder

¼ ground fenugreek seeds

Salt and ground black pepper to taste

1 lb pancetta slices

3 lb ground beef

2 large eggs, lightly beaten

1 cup fresh bread crumbs

1 cup tomato sauce

Directions

Preheat your electric smoker to 225°F by adding hickory smoker chips. Preheat a large cast-iron skillet on a smoking rack and pour in the olive oil. Add the onion, garlic, thyme, mustard powder, fenugreek seeds, salt, and pepper and stir to coat with the oil.

Smoke for 10-15 minutes until slightly browned. Take out the skillet from the heat and pour the ingredients into a stainless steel bowl. Leave them to cool.

In a large mixing bowl, thoroughly combine the beef, eggs, bread crumbs, tomato sauce, salt, and pepper. Add the onion mixture and mix well. Shape the mixture into a meatloaf. Wrap the meatloaf in the pancetta slices and transfer it to a smoking rack.

Smoke for about 2 hours or until a meat thermometer reads an internal temperature of 165°F. Remove the meatloaf from the heat and let it rest covered with foil for 10 minutes. Serve sliced.

Chipotle Tomahawk Ribeye Steaks

Prep Time: 40 minutes + marinating time | Cook Time: about 2 hours | Serves 4

Ingredients

3 tbsp honey

2 tbsp smoked paprika

1 tbsp garlic powder

1 tbsp mustard powder

Salt and ground black pepper to taste

1 tbsp dried thyme

1 tsp dried sage, crushed

1 tsp ground coriander

½ tsp chipotle powder

1 tsp ground cumin

2 tomahawk rib eye steaks

Directions

Place the honey, paprika, garlic, mustard, salt, pepper, thyme, sage, coriander, chipotle, and cumin in a bowl and whisk well to combine. Rub the steaks with the rub on all sides.

Place the steaks in a resealable bag, then remove as much air as possible before sealing it. Marinate in the refrigerator for 12 -24 hours.

Preheat your electric smoker to 275°F and add wood chips. Pull out the steaks of the refrigerator and put them on the smoking rack. Smoke for about 2 hours or until the internal thermometer reads 125°F for rare, 135°F for medium-rare, and 160°F for well-done. Let the steaks rest loosely covered with foil for 15-20 minutes.

Delicious Roast Beef Hash

Prep Time: 30 minutes | Cook Time: about 2 hours | Serves 4

Ingredients

2 tbsp olive oil

2 tbsp unsalted butter

2 lb eye of round roast, trimmed

Sea salt and black pepper to taste

1 tsp Hungarian sweet paprika

¼ tsp mushroom powder

¼ tsp ground nutmeg

4 Yukon gold potatoes, blanched and cubed

1 celery stalk, chopped

2 onion shallots, diced

1 red bell pepper, diced

4 garlic cloves, minced

4 thyme sprigs, leaves stripped

2 corn ears, kernels cut off

2 tbsp parsley, finely chopped

8 large eggs

Directions

Preheat your electric smoker to 250°F and add mild flavor wood chips. Coat the roast with salt, pepper, paprika, mushroom powder, and nutmeg and transfer it to a smoking rack. Smoke for 25-30 minutes.

Preheat a large cast-iron skillet by placing it on a smoking rack, then pour in the olive oil and butter. Add the potatoes, celery, shallots, bell pepper, garlic, thyme, salt, and pepper and stir well. Smoke for 90 minutes. Slide out the skillet and the roast from the heat.

Place the beef on a cutting board. Leave it to rest for 20 minutes before chopping it into small pieces. Transfer them to the skillet and add the corn; toss to incorporate.

Make small holes and crack an egg into each. Sprinkle with salt and pepper. Place the skillet back into the smoker and cook until the eggs are cooked. Serve topped with parsley.

Cholula Beef Quesadillas

Prep Time: 45 minutes | Cook Time: about 2 hours | Serves 8

Ingredients

5 tbsp olive oil

4 shallots, diced

8 scallions, finely sliced

2 red bell peppers, diced

Salt and ground black pepper to taste

2 lb chuck roast, trimmed and ground

2 tbsp red chili flakes

2 tbsp ground cumin

1 tbsp ground coriander

1 tbsp paprika

1 tbsp garlic powder

¼ tsp jalapeño powder

1 (12-oz) bottle pilsner beer

16 flour tortillas

2 lb Monterey Jack cheese, shredded

2 cups canned spicy black beans

3 tbsp Cholula hot sauce

1 cup pico de gallo

Directions

Preheat your electric smoker to 275°F and add mild flavor wood chips. Preheat a large cast-iron saucepan by placing it on a smoking rack, then pour in 2 tbsp of olive oil. Add the shallots, scallions, red bell peppers, salt, and pepper. Stir and smoke for 20 minutes.

Then, add the ground beef and sprinkle with red chili flakes, cumin, coriander, paprika, garlic powder, jalapeño powder, salt, and pepper. Smoke the beef for 20 minutes.

Deglaze the saucepan by pouring in the pilsner beer. Scrap up any browned bits from the bottom. Smoke for 10 minutes until the liquid is absorbed and the bottom of the pan is almost dry. Pull off the skillet from the smoker and allow the cooking liquid to cool slightly.

Coat half of the tortillas with 1 tbsp of olive oil. Divide the beef mixture, Monterey Jack cheese, and black beans between them and top with the remaining tortillas. Brush the tops with the remaining olive oil and season with salt and pepper.

Arrange the quesadillas on smoking racks and smoke them for 10-15 minutes until crispy. Cut the quesadillas into wedges and serve with Cholula hot sauce and pico de gallo.

Mozzarella Smoked T-Bone

Prep Time: 40 minutes + marinating time | Cooking Time: 4 hours | Serves: 4

Ingredients

4 (16 oz) T-bone steaks

1 cup prime rib rub mixture

1 cup mozzarella cheese, shredded

Directions

Rub meat with prime rib rub and wrap it into plastic wrap. Put in the refrigerator for 1 hour. Preheat your electric smoker to 225°F by adding apple wood chips. Take the steaks out of the refrigerator and remove the plastic wrap.

Arrange them onto a large baking rack and place them in the smoker. Cook the steaks for 35-45 minutes or until internal temperature reaches 115°F. Top with mozzarella cheese.

Chili Beef Short Ribs with Cipollini Onions

Prep Time: 40 minutes | Cook Time: 4 hours | Serves 4

Ingredients

2 tbsp olive oil
2 lb Cipollini onions, peeled
1 diced carrot
1 diced celery stalk
1 diced yellow onion
1 chili pepper, minced

1 tsp beef seasoning
2 lb beef short ribs, membrane removed
Salt and ground black pepper to taste
2 cups red wine
2 fresh bay leaves
4 cups vegetable stock

Directions

Preheat your electric smoker to 225°F by adding hickory smoker chips. Season the beef ribs on all sides with beef seasoning; set them aside. Preheat a large casserole on a smoking rack and pour in the olive oil. Add the Cipollini onions, carrot, celery, yellow onion, chili pepper, salt, and pepper and stir to coat them with the oil.

Smoke for 25-30 minutes until tender. Deglaze the casserole by pouring the red wine and scraping up any browned bits from the bottom. Stir in the bay leaves and vegetable stock. Place the ribs into the casserole and add the casserole back to the heat.

Smoke the ribs for 2-3 hours, brushing them with cooking juices every 25-30 minutes until the meat of the ribs falls easily from the bones. Take out the casserole from the heat.

Remove the ribs and Cipollini onions to a plate and cover them with aluminium foil. Strain the cooking juices through a sieve into a bowl and discard the solids.

Add the ribs and Cipollini onions back to the casserole and pour the strained liquid over. Continue smoking until the desired consistency of the sauce is achieved. Cut the ribs into individual bones and pour the sauce over them. Serve and enjoy!

Red Wine Beer Beef Stew

Prep Time: 40 minutes | Cook Time: 4 hours | Serves 8

Ingredients

4 tbsp unsalted butter

3 lb stewing beef, cubed

3 tbsp all-purpose flour

Salt and ground black pepper to taste

3 tbsp tomato paste

2 diced carrots

2 diced celery stalks

2 cups diced shallots

2 cups leeks, thinly sliced

3 garlic cloves, minced

1 cup red wine

1 cup vegetable broth

1 tbsp fresh thyme, chopped

3 fresh bay leaves

1 tbsp parsley, chopped

Directions

Preheat your electric smoker to 250°F and add mild flavor wood chips. Preheat a large cast-iron saucepan by placing it on a smoking rack, then place in the butter to melt.

Season the beef with salt and pepper and coat it in flour. Add the beef to the preheated saucepan and smoke for 20 minutes.

Slide out the saucepan and remove the meat. To the saucepan, add the tomato paste, carrots, celery, shallots, leeks, and garlic. Stir to coat and smoke for 20 minutes more.

Pour in the red wine to deglaze the saucepan, scraping up any browned bits from the bottom and add vegetable broth, thyme, and bay leaves.

Return the beef and continue smoking for 2-3 hours until the meat is tender. Remove and discard the bay leaves. Scatter with parsley and serve.

Italian Standing Rib Roast

Prep Time: 40 minutes | Cook Time: 4 hours | Serves 4

Ingredients

1 garlic bulb, cloves separated, peeled, and halved

4 lb bone-in standing rib roast, trimmed

4 tbsp rosemary, chopped

2 tbsp Italian seasoning

1 tbsp paprika

1 tbsp shallot powder

1 tbsp fennel powder

3 tbsp olive oil

Salt and ground black pepper to taste

Directions

Preheat your electric smoker to 275°F and add mild flavor wood chips. Place the roast on a clean flat surface, cut a few deep incisions, and stuff the holes with the garlic halves.

Mix the rosemary, Italian seasoning, paprika, shallot powder, fennel powder, salt, and pepper. Sprinkle the meat with olive oil and massage the spice mixture over the beef using your hands.

Transfer the roast, fat-side up, to a smoking rack and smoke for 3-4 hours or until the internal thermometer reads 160°F for well-done. Remove the roast from the heat to a cutting board and allow cooling for 5-10 minutes. Then, cut it into slices and serve.

Italian-Style Philly Cheesesteak

Prep Time: 45 minutes | Cook Time: about 2 hours | Serves 4

Ingredients

2 tbsp olive oil, divided

2 lb top round beef roast, trimmed

Salt and ground black pepper to taste

12 baby portobello mushrooms, sliced

2 tbsp Italian seasoning

2 white onions, very thinly sliced

1 green bell pepper, cored and thinly sliced

1 red bell pepper, cored, seeded, and sliced

4 garlic cloves, minced

¼ small fennel bulb, sliced

4 ciabatta rolls

8 Asiago cheese slices

Directions

Preheat your electric smoker to 275°F and add mild flavor wood chips. Sprinkle the beef roast with salt and pepper and put it on a smoking rack. Smoke for about 2 hours or until the internal thermometer reads 125°F for rare, 135°F for medium-rare, and 160°F for well-done.

Meanwhile, preheat a large cast-iron pan by placing it on a smoking rack, then pour in the olive oil. Add the mushrooms and Italian seasoning; toss to coat. Smoke for 20 minutes.

Remove the vegetables from the skillet and set them aside. Add the onions, bell peppers, garlic, fennel, salt, and pepper and stir with a spatula. Smoke for 18-20 minutes.

When the beef is ready, transfer it to a cutting board and allow it to rest loosely covered with foil for 15-20 minutes. Then, cut it into slices. To the onion mixture, add the mushrooms and stir.

Cover the Ciabatta rolls with beef slices and vegetables. Top with Asiago cheese slices. Put the sandwiches on smoking racks and smoke them for 8-10 minutes until the cheese melts.

Jalapeño Butcher's Steak (Hanger Steak)

Prep Time: 40 minutes + marinating time | Cook Time: about 1 hour | Serves 4

Ingredients

1 yellow onion, finely diced

1 tbsp grated fresh ginger

½ finely diced jalapeño pepper

3 garlic cloves, minced

2 tbsp soy sauce

2 tbsp oyster sauce

2 tbsp dark brown sugar

2 tbsp toasted sesame oil

2 tbsp olive oil

2 butcher's steak

Salt and ground black pepper to taste

Directions

Combine the yellow onion, ginger, jalapeño, garlic, soy sauce, oyster sauce, sugar, sesame oil, and olive oil in a mixing bowl and pour the mixture into a large resealable bag, then add the steaks. Remove as much air as possible from the bag before sealing it. Place the bag in the refrigerator for 12 hours, turning twice.

Preheat your electric smoker to 275°F. Add wood chips to begin the smoke. Remove the steaks, keeping the marinade in the refrigerator. Pat them dry with kitchen towels and sprinkle them with salt and pepper on both sides. Brush the beef with the reserved marinade.

Smoke the meat for another 25-30 minutes or until the internal thermometer reads 125°F for rare, 135°F for medium-rare, and 160°F for well-done. Once ready, let the steaks rest loosely covered with foil for 15-20 minutes. Serve and enjoy!

Herby T-bone Steak with Roasted Garlic

Prep Time: 40 minutes | Cook Time: about 2 hours | Serves 4

Ingredients

¼ cup olive oil

4 (2-inch-thick) porterhouse steaks

2 tbsp rosemary, chopped

2 tbsp thyme, chopped

1 tsp steak seasoning

5 garlic bulbs, tops cut off

4 tbsp unsalted butter

Directions

Preheat your electric smoker to 275°F and add apple wood chips. Drizzle the steaks with half of the olive oil and rub them with rosemary, thyme, and steak seasoning.

Sit the garlic bulbs on a foil and drizzle with the remaining olive oil. Sprinkle with salt and pepper. Put the steaks and garlic on the smoking racks. Smoke for about 2 hours, or until the internal thermometer reaches 135°F for medium-rare.

Remove the steaks to a cutting board and leave them to rest, loosely covered with foil, for 15-20minutes. Top the steaks with butter and serve with a roasted garlic bulb on the side.

Buttery Smoked New York Steaks with Parsley

Prep Time: 40 minutes + marinating time | Cooking Time: 70 minutes | Serves: 4

Ingredients

4 tbsp salted butter, softened
2 green onions, finely chopped.
½ tbsp salt
1 tbsp pepper

2 tbsp parsley, chopped
1 tbsp smoked paprika
2 tbsp red wine vinegar
2 (2-inch thick) New York strip steaks

Directions

Combine the green onions, parsley, butter, salt, pepper, paprika, and vinegar in a bowl and stir. Add steaks and toss to coat. Cover this mixture with plastic wrap, then place it in the refrigerator until the butter hardens.

Preheat your electric smoker to 225°F and add wood chips. Transfer the marinated steak to the smoking racks and smoke it for about 1 hour or until the internal temperature reaches 145°F for medium rare. Once smoking is done, remove the steaks. Let them rest for 10 minutes, then slice them. Serve and enjoy! Yummy!

Texas-Style Brisket

Prep Time: 40 minutes | Cooking Time: 90 minutes | Serves: 1

Ingredients

1 lb brisket
⅓ tbsp salt

½ tsp black pepper
2 tbsp lime juice

Directions

First, mix salt, lime juice, and pepper in a small bowl. Pour it all over the brisket. Preheat smoker temperature to 225°F. Add the apple wood chips and wait until smoke starts to build. Cook for about 90 minutes. Then serve.

Beef Tenderloin with Herbs

Prep Time: 40 minutes + marinating time | Cook Time: about 2 hours | Serves 4

Ingredients

2 yellow onions, sliced

1 tbsp thyme, chopped

1 tbsp rosemary, chopped

1 tbsp parsley, chopped

1 tbsp tarragon, chopped

¼ cup Dijon mustard

3 tbsp olive oil

2 tbsp ground cumin seeds

2 tbsp ground celery seeds

2 tbsp ground coriander seeds

Salt and ground black pepper to taste

1 center-cut beef tenderloin

Directions

Whisk the onions, thyme, rosemary, parsley, tarragon, mustard, and oil in a bowl. Stir in cumin, celery, coriander, salt, and pepper until smooth paste forms. Apply the herb paste onto the surface of the tenderloin, then wrap it tightly in cling film. Place in the fridge for 3-4 hours.

Preheat your electric smoker to 275°F and add mild flavor wood chips. Take out the meat from the fridge and remove the cling film. Smoke for about 2 hours or until the internal thermometer reads 125°F for rare, 135°F for medium-rare, and 160°F for well-done. Let the tenderloin rest loosely with foil for 15-20 minutes when done. Serve and enjoy!

Tangy Braised Beef Brisket

Prep Time: 40 minutes + marinating time | Cook Time: 8 hours | Serves 8

Ingredients

2 tbsp ancho chili powder

2 tbsp smoked paprika

2 tbsp fine sea salt

1 tbsp jeera (ground cumin)

1 tbsp mustard powder

1 (7-lb) beef brisket, trimmed

3 tbsp dark brown sugar

1 tsp garlic powder

1 tsp onion powder

1 tsp Tajín seasoning

Flaked sea salt and black pepper to taste

2 tbsp parsley, chopped for garnish

Directions

Mix the sugar, ancho chili powder, paprika, sea salt, jeera, mustard powder, garlic powder, onion powder, and Tajín seasoning. Apply the resulting spice mix by rubbing the brisket on all sides, then wrap it tightly in cling film. Place in the refrigerator for 12-24 hours.

Preheat your electric smoker to 200°F and add wood chips. Remove the meat from the refrigerator and season it all over with flaked sea salt and pepper. Smoke it on the smoking rack for 5 hours. Slide out the beef from the heat and place it on aluminum foil, then wrap it to form a packet.

Place the packet on a baking dish and add it to the smoker. Cook the brisket for about another 3 hours or until the internal temperature is reached 190°F. When ready, let the steaks rest loosely covered with foil for 25-30 minutes. Serve sliced and enjoy!

Paprika & Lemon Beef Ribs

Prep Time: 40 minutes | Cooking Time: 3 hours | Serves: 2

Ingredients

2 tbsp brown sugar

2 garlic cloves, minced

1 tbsp paprika

2 tbsp onion powder

2 lb beef ribs

3 tbsp lemon juice

Directions

Preheat your smoker to200°F. Mix the brown sugar, garlic, paprika, and onion powder in a large bowl. Sprinkle the spice mixture over the beef ribs. Rub well for fine coating.

Next, smoke it in an electric smoker for 3 hours at 250°F. After 2 hours, take out the ribs and pour lemon juice on top. Serve warm.

Five-Spice Smoked Brisket

Prep Time: 40 minutes + marinating time | Cooking Time: 3 hours | Serves: 3

Ingredients

2 lb beef brisket

Salt and black pepper to taste

1 tsp garlic paste

1 tsp ginger paste

½ tsp lemon juice

2 pinch five-spice powder

Directions

Cut the brisket into pieces. Mix all the remaining listed together in a bowl. Coat the brisket with the mixture. Put the brisket in the fridge for 1 hour.

Preheat your electric smoker to 225°F. Remove the brisket from the refrigerator and transfer it to the electric smoker. Cook for 3 hours. Serve and enjoy!

Sweet Baby Back Ribs

Prep Time: 120 minutes | Cooking Time: 90 minutes | Serves: 3

Ingredients

2 tbsp salt

3 slabs baby back ribs

Sauce ingredients

3 cups tomato ketchup

¼ cup apple vinegar

3 tbsp lemon juice

2 tbsp garlic powder

½ tbsp onion powder

2 tbsp garlic pepper

Directions

Sprinkle the baby back ribs with a generous amount of salt. Combine all the sauce ingredients in a separate bowl and set aside.

Preheat your electric smoker to 260°F. Cover the meat with the glaze. Place it on a baking rack and smoker in the electric smoker for 90 minutes at 200°F. Serve and enjoy by pouring the remaining sauce on top.

Red Wine Beef Sirloin

Prep Time: 40 minutes + marinating time | Cooking Time: 4-5 hours | Serves: 4

Ingredients

4 lb beef sirloin

Salt and black pepper to taste

2 tbsp vegetable oil

1 cup red wine

310 mL beef consommé

2 tbsp butter

Directions

Preheat your electric smoker to 225°F by adding apple wood chips. Sprinkle the meat with salt and pepper and rub the vegetable oil on top. Put the meat in the electric smoker and cook for 4-5 hours.

Meanwhile, take a saucepan and add butter. Let it melt, pour in the red wine and cook until a boil comes. Add the beef consommé. Once smooth and light, the sauce is ready. Turn off the heat.

Take out the beef sirloin from the smoker and let it stand at room temperature for 20 minutes. Cut the meat and serve it by pouring the sauce over the top.

Rosemary Beef Prime Rib with BBQ Sauce

Prep Time: 40 minutes + marinating time | Cooking Time: 4 hours 30 minutes | Serves: 4

Ingredients

3 lb beef prime rib, bone removed

2-3 tbsp olive oil

½ tbsp salt

½ tbsp black pepper

1 tsp paprika

½ tsp cayenne pepper

½ tsp thyme

1 tsp onion powder

1 tsp rosemary

1 cup BBQ sauce

Directions

Combine the oil, salt, black pepper, paprika, cayenne pepper, thyme, onion powder, and rosemary in a bowl and mix well. Rub it gently over the prime rib. Let it sit for 1 hour.

Meanwhile, Preheat your electric smoker to 200°F for 2 hours. Then, smoke the meat inside the smoker for 4 hours and a half-hour. Afterward, serve it with BBQ sauce.

Garlic Mustard Smoked Beef Tenderloin

Prep Time: 40 minutes + marinating time | Cooking Time: 3 hours 30 minutes | Serves: 3

Ingredients

3 lb beef tenderloin

2 butter sticks, cubed

Sea salt and black pepper to taste

Baste ingredients

10 garlic cloves, minced

⅓ cup parsley, chopped

½ cup rosemary, chopped

2 tsp English mustard

2 tsp honey

2 tbsp olive oil

6 oz Armagnac or brandy

Directions

Combine all the basting ingredients in a large pot and submerge the beef for 4 hours. Afterward, remove the tenderloin from the basting mixture and let it sit at room temperature for a few minutes. Rub salt and pepper gently over the beef tenderloin for a fine coating.

Smoke on top of most racks for a half-hour at 225°F by adding apple wood chips. Afterward, transfer it to the plate and rub 2 sticks of butter. Seal it with aluminum foil and cook for 3 hours at 225°F. Serve.

Roast Lamb with Honey Mustard Glaze

Prep Time: 40 minutes + marinating time | Cooking Time: 3 and ½ hours | Serves: 4

Ingredients

2 lb lamb shoulder

Brine ingredients

2 tsp salt

1 tsp vinegar

1 tsp garlic powder

1 tsp onion powder

4 cups water

Glaze ingredients

1 cup honey

½ cup soy sauce

⅓ cup mustard

Salt and black pepper to taste

Directions

Mix all the brine ingredients in a large pot. Cut the lamb into pieces. Submerge the lamb in the brine mixture for 6 hours. Take out the lamb and pat dry. Let it dry at room temperature.

Preheat your electric smoker to 225°F. Put the lamb in the smoker and cook it for 3 hours. Mix all the glaze ingredients in a small mixing bowl. After 3 hours, drizzle honey glaze on top. Put the lamb again in a smoker at 175°F for half-hour.

Lime & Mustard Brisket

Prep Time: 40 minutes + marinating time | Cooking Time: 5 hours | Serves: 3

Ingredients

1 tsp paprika

1 tsp dried mustard

½ tsp thyme

2 tsp lime juice

1 tsp salt

3 lb brisket

Directions

Mix paprika, dried mustard, thyme, lime juice, and salt together in a bowl. Massage the mixture all over the brisket for fine coating. Let it marinate for 2 hours.

Preheat your electric smoker to 230°F by adding apple wood chips. Put the brisket in the smoker and cook it for about 5 hours or until the internal thermometer reads 160°F for well-done. Let the brisket rest loosely with foil for a few minutes when done. Serve.

Lamb Rib Chops with BBQ Sauce

Prep Time: 40 minutes + marinating time | Cooking Time: 3 hours | Serves: 4

Ingredients

2 lb lamb rib chops

Salt and black pepper to taste

2 tsp BBQ Sauce

2 tsp apple vinegar

1 tsp thyme

2 tsp garlic powder

½ tsp onion powder

1 tsp ketchup

Directions

Combine all the listed ingredients in a bowl to make a glaze, excluding meat. Pour the glaze on the lamb chops and transfer them to the plastic zip-lock bag. Place in the fridge for 2 hours before starting cooking.

Preheat your smoker to 225°F by adding apple wood chips. Remove the lamb from the fridge and put it in the smoker. Cook for 3 hours at 225°F. Brush the dripping on top and serve.

Lamb Chops with Honey-Balsamic Glaze

Prep Time: 40 minutes + marinating time | Cooking Time: 3 hours | Serves: 4

Ingredients

12 lamb chops

4 tsp honey

2 tsp balsamic vinegar

Dry spices

½ tsp salt

½ tsp paprika

¼ tsp garlic powder

1 tsp dried mustard

½ tsp thyme

Directions

Cut the lamb into pieces with a sharp knife. Mix all dry spices in a large bowl. Rub the spices on the lamb and massage for fine coating.

Place the lamb in a zip-lock plastic bag and then marinate in the refrigerator for 1 hour. Add the marinated lamb to a greased skillet. Cook in the smoker at 220°F for 3 hours. Drizzle some honey and vinegar at the end after taking out the lamb for a bit o sweetness.

Teriyaki Beef

Prep Time: 40 minutes + marinating time | Cooking Time: 4 hours | Serves: 4

Ingredients

3 lb thinly sliced beef

½ cup teriyaki sauce

2 cups brown sugar

2 tbsp ginger paste

2 tbsp onion powder

2 tbsp lemon juice

Directions

Mix teriyaki sauce, brown sugar, ginger paste, onion powder, and lemon juice in a large bowl. Rub it over the beef. Let it stand for 1 hour in the fridge.

Place apple wood chips into the smoker and let it preheat to 225°F for 30 minutes. Now smoke the lamb by placing it on the topmost rack of the smoker for 4 hours. Serve.

Delicious Rib-Eye Steak

Prep Time: 40 minutes + marinating time | Cooking Time: 4 hours | Serves: 4

Ingredients

4 rib-eye steak, 2-inches thick

2 cups sharp cheddar cheese, grated

1 tsp black pepper

3 tbsp chipotle powder

½ tbsp paprika

½ cup olive oil

Directions

Combine the entire spice ingredients in a bowl. Rub the mixture all over the meat. Let it sit for 2 hours. Afterward, put the steaks in the electric smoker for 4 hours at 225°F. After 4 hours, take out the lamb and sprinkle cheese on top. Let the cheese get melted, and serve.

Saucy Leg of Lamb with Herbs

Prep Time: 40 minutes + marinating time | Cooking Time: 8 hours | Serves: 8

Ingredients

6 lb leg of lamb, boneless

½ cup olive oil

4 tsp fresh rosemary, chopped

5 tsp fresh thyme, chopped

10 tsp BBQ sauce

1 tsp garlic powder

Directions

Rub ½ cup of olive oil on the leg of lamb. Mix the rosemary, garlic powder and fresh thyme in a bowl. Rub this mixture onto the leg of lamb. Put it in the refrigerator for 1 hour.

Preheat your smoker to 225°F. Remove the lamb from the refrigerator and put it in the smoker. Smoke for 8 hours, drizzling it with BBQ sauce every 2 hours. Serve and enjoy!

Rack of Lamb with Lemon

Prep Time: 40 minutes | Cooking Time: 3 hours | Serves: 3

Ingredients

2 lb rack of lamb

1 lemon, juiced

1 cup BBQ sauce

1 tsp onion powder

2 tsp thyme

Garlic salt and black pepper to taste

Directions

Mix the onion powder, thyme, garlic salt, and pepper in a small bowl and then rub the mixture over the meat. Then put the lamb onto a baking dish and place it in your smoker. Smoke for 3 hours at 260°F. Mix lemon juice and BBQ sauce in a bowl. At the 2-hour mark, brush the lamb with the BBQ glaze. Cook for the remaining 1 hour. Serve and enjoy.

Chinese-Style Lamb Shoulder

Prep Time: 40 minutes + marinating time | Cooking Time: 7 hours | Serves: 6

Ingredients

3 lb boneless lamb shoulder

1 tbsp five-spice powder

2 tsp dark brown sugar

Sea salt to taste

Char Siu Sauce

¼ cup hoisin sauce

2 tsp honey

3 tbsp soy sauce

¼ cup dry sherry

Directions

Preheat your electric smoker to 255°F. Then add wood chips. Rub the lamb in a bowl. Rub the lamb with five-spice powder, brown sugar, and salt. Smoke it for 7 hours.

Pour the sauce ingredients into a saucepan over medium heat. Simmer the sauce for 10 minutes until thickened. Brush the lamb with the sauce every 2 hours. Serve.

PORK RECIPES

Spiced Pork Baby Back Ribs

Prep Time: 40 minutes | Cook Time: about 4 hours | Serves 4

Ingredients

8 lb baby back pork ribs, membranes removed

2 cups honey

2 cups packed dark brown sugar

2 cups dark molasses

2 cups white wine vinegar

½ cup brandy

Spices

1 tbsp celery seeds, whole

3 tbsp cumin seeds, whole

3 tbsp coriander seeds, whole

1 tbsp allspice berries, whole

3 tbsp smoked paprika

3 tbsp ancho chili powder

1 tbsp mustard powder

1 tbsp garlic powder

1 tbsp onion powder

Salt and ground black pepper to taste

Directions

Preheat your electric smoker to 250°F by adding in mild or any other wood chips. Combine all the spice ingredients in a bowl and rub the resulting mixture all over the rib sides. Transfer them to smoking trays, flesh-side up. Smoke the ribs for about 2 hours.

Mix the honey, brown sugar, and molasses in a bowl until well incorporated. Take a piece of aluminium foil and fold it into a rectangular shape. Remove the ribs from the smoker to the foil and brush them with the sweet mixture. Add the white wine vinegar and brandy.

Wrap the foil into a parcel and place it in the smoker. Smoke for another 2 hours. Leave the ribs to sit for 15-20 minutes. Unwrap and serve drizzled with some of the foil juices.

Herby Pork Chops with Tender Pears

Prep Time: 40 minutes | Cook Time: 1 hour 30 minutes | Serves 4

Ingredients

1 tbsp olive oil

1 tbsp unsalted butter

4 bone-in pork chops

¼ tsp garlic powder

Salt and ground black pepper to taste
¼ cup smoked paprika
2 fresh thyme sprigs

2 sage sprigs
3 pears, halved and cored
2 lemons, halved

Directions

Preheat the electric smoker to 275°F by adding mild or wood chips. Preheat a large cast-iron skillet by placing it on a smoking rack, then add the butter to melt. Rub the pork chops with olive oil. Season with garlic powder, salt, pepper, and paprika.

Press the thyme and sage sprigs into the slippery surface of the chops and put them, herb-side down, on the smoking rack. Smoke for 60-90 minutes until a meat thermometer reads an internal temperature of 145°F. Add the pears to the skillet, flesh-side down.

Cook for 18-20 minutes until tender. Remove and set aside. Transfer the pork to a cutting board and leave it to rest for 10-15 minutes, loosely covered with aluminum foil. Pour the cooking juices over the chops. Serve with thinly sliced pear and lemon halves for squeezing.

Sticky Garam Masala Spareribs

Prep Time: 40 minutes | Cook Time: about 4 hours | Serves 4

Ingredients

2 tbsp garam masala
6 lb pork spareribs, membranes removed
Salt and ground black pepper to taste
½ cup mirin
2 oranges, juiced and zested

4 garlic cloves, minced
3 tbsp honey
3 tbsp tamari sauce
3 tbsp hoisin sauce
3 tbsp dark brown sugar

Directions

Preheat your electric smoker to 250°F by adding mild or wood chips. Rub the garam masala evenly over all sides of the ribs and sprinkle them with salt and pepper. Place the ribs on smoking trays, flesh-side up and smoke for about 2 hours.

Mix the mirin, orange zest, orange juice, garlic, honey, tamari sauce, hoisin sauce, and brown sugar in a medium bowl. Transfer to a baking sheet. Add the ribs, flesh-side down and cover with aluminium foil.

Smoke for another 2 hours until the meat is tender. Take the ribs out from the smoker and leave them to rest, covered, for 15-20 minutes. Remove the foil and cut the ribs into individual bones. Serve topped with the cooking juices.

Pork Ragú a la Bolognese

Prep Time: 40 minutes + marinating time | Cook Time: about 4 hours | Serves 8

Ingredients

2 lb pork Boston butt, trimmed

¼ cup sea salt

2 tbsp fresh thyme, chopped

3 lemons, thinly sliced

3 fresh bay leaves

Salt and ground black pepper to taste

½ cup olive oil

1 diced white onion

4 garlic cloves, minced

1 diced carrot

1 diced celery stalk

2 cups red wine

4 cups passata

4 cups chicken broth

3 fresh bay leaves

1 tbsp Italian seasoning

¼ tsp ground nutmeg

1 lb dried pappardelle

3 tbsp grated Parmesan cheese

Directions

Dissolve the sea salt in 4 cups of water. Stir in the thyme, lemon slices, and bay leaves. Place the pork in a large resealable bag and pour in the brine and remove as much air as possible before sealing the bag. Place in refrigerator and marinate overnight.

Preheat your smoker to 250°F and add apple wood chips. Pull out the pork of the refrigerator. Remove and discard the marinade. Pat it dry with paper towels and sprinkle with salt and pepper. Place the pork on a smoking rack.

Warm the olive oil in a large saucepan in the smoker. Add the onion, garlic, carrot, celery, salt, and pepper and stir well. Smoke for 18-20 minutes, stirring periodically.

Deglaze the saucepan by adding the red wine and, using a spatula, scrape any bits stuck at the bottom. Stir in the passata, chicken broth, bay leaves, Italian seasoning, and nutmeg. Smoke for 55-60 minutes.

When the internal temperature of the pork reaches 190°F, the pork is ready. Remove the pork to a cutting board and cover it loosely with aluminum foil and let it cool slightly for about 40 minutes. Shred the pork with two forks and place it in the saucepan.

Smoke the mixture for 25-30 minutes until the sauce thickens. Get rid of the bay leaves. Adjust the seasoning with salt and pepper, as needed. Cook the pappardelle in lightly salted boiling water until 'al dente', 8-10 minutes. Drain and add to the saucepan. Stir well and serve topped with Parmesan cheese.

Chili Mustard Smoke Pork Tenderloin

Prep Time: 40 minutes | Cooking Time: 3 hours | Serves: 2

Ingredients

2 pork tenderloins

4 tbsp BBQ sauce

Rub ingredients

¼ cup cane sugar

¼ tsp chili powder

½ tbsp granulated onion

½ tbsp granulated garlic

½ tbsp dried chilies

¼ tbsp dill weed

½ tbsp lemon powder

½ tbsp mustard powder

Directions

Add apple wood chips to your smoker and adjust the setting to 225°F. Trim the pork fat and silver skin. Combine all the rub ingredients in a large bowl and rub the resulting seasoning onto the pork loin. Place the pork in the smoker. Cook for 3 hours until internal temperate reaches 200°F. Brush the BBQ sauce on the pork and then leave it to sit for 20 minutes.

Prosciutto Stuffed Pork Tenderloin

Prep Time: 40 minutes | Cooking Time: 2-3 hours | Serves: 6

Ingredients

2 lb tenderloin, trimmed

½ cup prosciutto slices

¼ cup fresh bread crumbs

3 tbsp fresh parsley, minced

1 tsp fresh rosemary, minced

2 garlic cloves, minced

4 tbsp extra virgin olive oil

Salt and black pepper to taste

Directions

Preheat your electric smoker to 225°F by adding the cherry wood chips into the smoker box. Put the tenderloins on a cutting board. Place the prosciutto slices over one of the tenderloins so it hangs from all sides. In a bowl, combine bread crumbs, rosemary, parsley, and garlic.

Place it over the prosciutto. Lay tenderloin on top and then ties it with kitchen string. Transfer the meat to a foil-lined baking sheet.

Insert it into the smoker. Attach the digital thermometer to read the temperate. Smoke until it reaches the internal temperature of 205°F. Let the tenderloin rest 20 minutes before removing the string. Serve sliced.

Tasty Pork Chops with Potatoes & Beans

Prep Time: 40 minutes | Cook Time: about 2 hours | Serves 4

Ingredients

3 tbsp olive oil

4 bone-in pork chops

Salt and ground black pepper to taste

4 leeks, thinly sliced

1 garlic bulb, halved

8 fingerling potatoes, halved lengthwise

1 cup white wine

1 cup vegetable stock

4 cups kidney beans, drained and rinsed

2 tbsp parsley, chopped

1 lemon, juiced and zested

2 tbsp thyme, chopped

Directions

Preheat your electric smoker to 275°F by adding mild or wood chips. Add 2 tablespoons of olive oil to a large cast-iron skillet. Gently brush the chops with the remaining olive oil, then season them with salt and pepper on both sides. Place them on a smoking rack. Smoke the pork chops for 55-60 minutes.

Add the leeks, garlic, fingerling potatoes, thyme, salt, and pepper to the skillet and stir well to coat in the olive oil. Pour in the white wine, vegetable stock, kidney beans, parsley, lemon zest, and juice. Sprinkle with salt and pepper. Smoke for 55-60 minutes. Give everything a good stir, and using a wooden spoon.

Make 4 wells in the bean mixture. Place the chops in each space and smoke for another 55-60 minutes until the internal temperature of the meat reaches 145°F. Remove the skillet from the heat and let it rest for 10 minutes. Serve garnished with thyme, and enjoy.

Home-Style Smoked Maple Bacon

Prep Time: 40 minutes + marinating time | Cook Time: 3 hours | Serves 20

Ingredients

1 tsp brown sugar

½ cup pure maple syrup

¼ cup coarse sea salt

3 garlic cloves, minced

3 fresh bay leaves, finely chopped

1 tbsp tarragon, chopped

2 tbsp thyme, chopped

2 tbsp rosemary, chopped

2 tbsp peppercorns, whole

2 tbsp fennel seeds, whole

3 tbsp caraway seeds, whole

1 tsp coriander seeds, whole

5 lb skin-on pork belly

Directions

Blitz the brown sugar, maple syrup, sea salt, garlic, bay leaves, tarragon, thyme, rosemary, peppercorns, fennel, caraway, and coriander seeds in your food processor until smooth.

Rub the pork belly with the resulting mixture, then place it in a large sealable plastic bag. Remove as much air as possible from the bag before sealing it. Place the bag in the refrigerator for 7 days turning 2-3 times.

Preheat your electric smoker to 200°F by adding mild or wood chips. Remove the pork from the refrigerator and rinse it with cold water. Pat it dry with kitchen towels.

Transfer the pork belly, skin-side up, to a smoking tray. Smoke for 2-3 hours, or until the internal temperature reaches 165°F. Remove the bacon to a cutting board and cover it with aluminum foil for 15-20 minutes before slicing and serving.

Chinese Pork Jowl

Prep Time: 40 minutes + marinating time | Cook Time: 3 hours | Serves 4

Ingredients

2 pork jowls, excess fat removed
½ tsp fish sauce
½ cup tamari sauce
2 cups rice wine
1 cup hoisin sauce
3 tbsp sesame oil

2 tbsp dark brown sugar
1 tbsp cilantro, chopped
2 tbsp honey
2 tsp Chinese five-spice powder
Salt and ground black pepper to taste

Directions

To prepare the pork jowls, score the fatty side of the pork fat. Then flip it over and cut the other side, which will provide space for the marinade to penetrate the meat. In a bowl, combine fish sauce, tamari, rice wine, hoisin, sesame oil, sugar, cilantro, honey, and five-spice powder.

Place the pork in a large sealable plastic bag with the marinade, removing as much air as possible from the bag; then seal it. Marinate in the refrigerator for 12-24 hours.

Preheat your smoker to 250°F. Add mild or wood chips. Take out the jowls of the bag, reserving the marinade for later in the refrigerator. Rub the pork jowl with salt and pepper and put it on a smoking rack. Smoke for 55-60 minutes. Use the reserved marinade to baste each jowl.

Continue smoking for another 55-60 minutes until the meat reaches an internal temperature of 165°F. Remove from the heat and loosely cover with aluminum foil for up to 20 minutes.

Crunchy Pork Belly with Pearl Onions

Prep Time: 40 minutes | Cook Time: about 4 hours | Serves 8

Ingredients

4 tbsp unsalted butter

4 lb pork belly, trimmed

3 tbsp fennel seeds, whole

2 tbsp thyme, chopped

1 tsp basil, finely chopped

1 tsp lemon zest

Salt and ground black pepper to taste

1 lb pearl onions, peeled

1 garlic clove, minced

3 fresh bay leaves

1 cup white wine

Directions

Preheat your electric smoker to 225°F by adding mild or wood chips. Put a large cast-iron skillet on a smoking rack and add the butter to melt. Mix the fennel seeds, thyme, basil, lemon zest, salt, and pepper in a small bowl. Use a very sharp knife to score the pork belly skin diagonally in a diamond pattern.

Season generously with the spice mixture, rubbing it well into the skin. Place the pork on the smoking rack, skin-side up and adjust the target temperature to 165°F. Add the pearl onions, garlic, and bay leaves to the butter and toss them to coat. Season with salt and pepper. Smoke for 20-25 minutes until tender.

Add the white wine and deglaze the skillet, stirring and scraping up any bits stuck at the bottom. Smoke the sauce for 15 more minutes. Remove and set aside. Continue smoking the pork belly until it reaches an internal temperature of 165°F. Then remove the pork and cover it loosely with aluminum foil; let it rest for 15-20 minutes. Slice the pork belly and spoon it over the warm sauce. Serve with pearl onions.

Tequila-Honey Smoked Ham

Prep Time: 40 minutes + marinating time | Cook Time: 5 hours | Serves 12

Ingredients

½ cup orange juice

¼ cup lemon juice

¼ cup lime juice

½ cup pineapple juice

¼ cup tequila

¼ cup honey

1 tsp dark brown sugar

¼ cup spicy brown mustard

1 (16-lb) bone-in pork butt (whole ham)

Salt and ground black pepper to taste

Directions

Combine orange, lemon, lime, pineapple, tequila, honey, brown sugar, and mustard in a bowl and whisk well. Pour the mixture into a large resealable plastic bag and add the pork. Shake to coat and seal the bag after removing as much air as possible from it. Marinate in the fridge for 12-24 hours, flipping 2-3 times.

Preheat your smoker to 225°F by adding mild or wood chips. Start by removing the pork from the brine and reserving the brine. Pat the pork dry with kitchen towels. Use a meat injector to syringe all the brine into several different spots in the pork. Sprinkle with salt and pepper.

Place the pork in a shallow dish and place it on a smoking rack. Smoke for 4-4 ½ hours until the internal temperature reaches 165°F, pouring the meat with the cooking juices halfway through the cooking. Remove the dish from the heat and let it rest for 50-60 minutes, loosely covered with foil, before slicing.

Spicy-Sweet Pork Shoulder

Prep Time: 40 minutes + marinating time | Cooking Time: 4 hours | Serves: 6

Ingredients

4 lb pork shoulder, roasts

Rub ingredients

¼ cup brown sugar

½ cup white sugar

½ cup paprika

⅓ cup garlic powder

1 tbsp chili powder

1 tsp cayenne pepper

1 tsp dried oregano

1 tsp cumin

Injection liquid ingredients

¾ cup apple juice

½ cup water

½ cup sugar

3 tbsp salt

2 tbsp Worcestershire sauce

Directions

Mix all the rub ingredients in a bowl. Blend all the liquid ingredients in a separate bowl. Inject the liquid into the meat using the injector. Pat dry the top surface of the meat, and then rub the spice mix all over the meat evenly. Let the meat sit for 2 hours at room temperature.

Preheat your smoker to 225°F and place apple wood chips in the smoke box. Place the pork in the smoker and cook for 4 hours or until it reaches the internal temperature of 205°F.

Yakitori (Japanese Pork Skewers)

Prep Time: 40 minutes + marinating time | Cook Time: 2 hours | Serves 4

Ingredients

½ tsp togarashi blend (Japanese spice seasoning)

½ cup soy sauce

1 cup oyster sauce

½ cup rice wine

½ cup sake

½ cup packed dark brown sugar

2 pork tenderloins, cubed

1 pineapple, diced

2 red bell peppers, diced

1 yellow onion, quartered

Directions

Pour the soy sauce, oyster sauce, rice wine, sake, togarashi blend, and brown sugar into a large sealable plastic bag and shake to combine. Add the pork cubes and massage them to coat. Seal the bag, making sure to remove as much air as possible. Marinate in the refrigerator for 24 hours, flipping 2-3 times.

Preheat your electric smoker to 225°F by adding mild or wood chips. Discard the pork, reserving the marinade for later. Alternate the pork cubes, pineapple, red pepper, and yellow onion on 8 bamboo skewers and arrange them on smoking trays. Brush them with the reserved marinade.

Smoke for 60-80 minutes, basting them with the remaining marinade every 15-20 minutes until the internal temperature is reached 165°F. Serve warm.

Pulled Pork Subs with Fennel Slaw

Prep Time: 40 minutes + marinating time | Cook Time: about 8 hours | Serves 8

Ingredients

4 cups lemon juice

12 garlic cloves, halved

3 white onions, very thinly sliced

1 serrano chili pepper, sliced

3-star anise, whole

3 thyme sprigs

3 rosemary sprigs

1 tbsp fennel seeds, whole

1 tbsp coriander seeds, whole

1 tbsp peppercorns

5 lb pork shoulder, trimmed

Fennel Slaw

1 fennel bulb, finely sliced

1 cabbage, trimmed, cored, and finely sliced

1 carrot, grated

2 tbsp honey

½ cup mayonnaise

½ cup apple cider vinegar

2 tbsp Dijon mustard

Salt and ground black pepper to taste

8 halved buttered sub rolls, grilled

Directions

Mix the lemon juice, garlic, onions, serrano chili, star anise, thyme, rosemary, fennel seeds, coriander seeds, and peppercorns in a bowl. Place the pork in a large sealable bag and add the marinade. Remove as much air as possible before sealing the bag. Place in refrigerator and marinate overnight.

Blend the honey, mayonnaise, vinegar, mustard, salt, and pepper in a bowl. Add the fennel, cabbage, and carrot to a salad bowl. Pour in the dressing and toss to coat. Cover and keep in the fridge until ready to use.

Preheat your electric smoker to 250°F by adding mild or wood chips. Remove the pork, pat it dry with paper towels, and put it in a shallow dish. Put the dish on a smoking rack.

Smoke for 5-6 hours until the internal temperature has reached 190°F. Remove the pork to a cutting board and let it rest covered for 15-20 minutes. Then, shred it with two forks. Divide the pulled pork and slaw between the sub rolls and serve.

Baby Back Ribs in Balsamic BBQ Sauce

Prep Time: 40 minutes | Cooking Time: 4 hours | Serves: 4

Ingredients

2 racks baby back ribs

1 ½ cups balsamic barbecue sauce

Rub ingredients

1 tbsp dark brown sugar

Salt and black pepper to taste

½ tbsp granulated sugar

2 tbsp paprika

⅓ tsp ground white pepper

1 tsp ground mustard

⅓ tsp dried thyme

½ tsp garlic powder

½ tsp ground Szechuan peppercorns

⅓ tsp cayenne pepper

Directions

Put on your electric smoker to preheat and add apple wood. Adjust the setting to 225°F. Combine all the rub ingredients in a large bowl. Season the ribs with the rub and set aside.

Once the wood starts giving smoke, place the ribs in the smoker. Smoke for 4 hours. When one hour is left, base the top of the ribs with the BBQ sauce. Continue to cook until caramelized.

Pork Loin Wrapped in Bacon

Prep Time: 40 minutes | Cook Time: 3 hours | Serves 8

Ingredients

4 tbsp unsalted butter

8 cups fresh spinach, stemmed and sliced

1 lb cremini mushrooms, sliced

8 garlic cloves, finely sliced

1 yellow onion, finely diced

1 red bell pepper, thinly sliced

1 Serrano pepper, thinly sliced

½ tsp hot paprika

Salt and ground black pepper to taste

1 pork loin, silver skin removed, trimmed

1 lb smoked bacon slices

Directions

Preheat your smoker to 250°F. Add hickory wood chips. Put a cast-iron dish on a smoking rack to preheat. Add the butter and let it melt. Stir in spinach, mushrooms, garlic, onion, bell pepper, Serrano pepper, paprika, salt, and pepper. Cook for 20-25 minutes until lightly browned.

While cooking, place the pork loin on a large cutting board and cut it by cutting lengthwise through it but not all the way through. Open it like a book, then remove the cast-iron dish from the smoker. Add all the ingredients to a medium stainless steel bowl to cool down.

Arrange the bacon strips on a large plastic wrap without overlapping. Salt and pepper the pork inside and out. Spoon the spinach stuffing onto the meat and roll it up to encase the filling.

Place the loin in the center of the bacon strips. Pull up each side tightly, using the plastic wrap and fully wrap the loin in the bacon. Transfer the pork to a smoking rack. Smoke for 2-3 hours or until a meat thermometer reads an internal temperature of 165°F. Take out the pork of the heat and loosely cover it with aluminum foil; let it sit for 20 minutes. Serve sliced.

Famous Memphis-Style Pork Ribs

Prep Time: 40 minutes + marinating time | Cook Time: 4 hours | Serves 4

Ingredients

2 (3-lb) racks St. Louis-cut pork spareribs, trimmed

6 tbsp dark brown sugar

2 tbsp smoked paprika

1 tbsp garlic powder

1 tbsp shallot powder

6 tbsp fine pink salt

Black pepper to taste

1 tsp dried thyme

1 tsp dried tarragon

1 tsp dried oregano

1 tsp ground cumin

1 tsp mustard powder
1 tsp ground fennel seeds
½ tsp chili powder

1 cup apple cider
1 cup white wine vinegar
¼ cup molasses

Directions

Mix together the brown sugar, smoked paprika, garlic powder, shallot powder, pink salt, black pepper, thyme, tarragon, oregano, cumin, mustard, fennel, and chili in a medium bowl. Season the ribs with half of the spice mix on both sides and massage them to coat well.

Wrap the ribs in plastic wrap and chill them for 12-24 hours. Whisk the remaining spice mix, apple cider, white wine vinegar, and molasses and set aside.

Preheat your smoker to 225°F. Add mild or wood chips. Place the ribs on smoking trays, flesh-side up. Smoke for 55-60 minutes. Brush them on both sides with the wine mixture.

Continue smoking for another 2-3 hours more, brushing the ribs every 30 minutes until the ribs are browned and sticky. Remove them from the heat and cover them with aluminum foil. Leave them to rest for 10 minutes, then serve.

BBQ Pork Chops

Prep Time: 40 minutes + marinating time | Cooking Time: 4 hours 20 minutes | Serves: 4

Ingredients

4 boneless pork chops
½ cup BBQ rub
2 tbsp canola oil
2 Spanish onions
2 Granny Smith apples

2 tbsp butter
¼ tsp cinnamon
½ tsp dry mustard
⅓ tsp nutmeg
Salt and black pepper to taste

Directions

Preheat your smoker to 225°F. Place apple wood chips in the smoke box. Season the pork chops with BBQ rub by placing them on a baking sheet. Cover with the aluminum foil.

Insert a digital thermometer in the thickest part of the pork chops. Set the internal temperate to 200°F. Place the baking sheets into the smoker. Smoke the chops for about 4 hours.

Heat the canola oil in a skillet overa a low flame. Add the onions and cook until soft, 15 minutes. Take out the onions. Add apples and 2 tbsp of water to the skillet; cook until golden.

Melt the butter in the same pan and add cinnamon, mustard, and nutmeg. Add onions back to the pan and mix well. Season with salt and pepper. Spoon the over the chops. Serve.

Tasty Ham with Sweet Maple Glaze

Prep Time: 40 minutes | Cooking Time: 3 hours 40 minutes | Serves: 4

Ingredients

4 lb boneless ham, sliced

Glaze ingredients

⅓ cup maple syrup

½ cup spicy honey

½ cup dark brown sugar

¼ cup ground red pepper

¼ cup apple juice

¼ tsp minced ginger

¼ tsp cinnamon

¼ tsp garlic powder

Directions

Preheat your smoker to 225°F. Take a small pot and heat it over medium flame. Add all the glaze ingredients to the cooking pot and let it cook for about 5 minutes. Once the sugar dissolves, the glaze is ready. Now place the ham in a casserole dish, cut side down.

Drizzle half of the glaze over the ham and brush it for an even coating. Cover the ham with foil tightly. Place the casserole on the middle rack of the electric smoker and cook it for 3 ½ hours.

Afterward, remove the ham from the electric smoker. Drain off the juices. At this stage, apply the reserved glaze over the ham. Replace wood chips with new fresh ones.

Put the ham back in the smoker uncovered when the smoke gets heavy. Let it cook for 10 more minutes. Remove the ham from the smoker; let it sit for 20 minutes. Slice and serve.

Dijon Pork Roast with White Wine Gravy

Prep Time: 40 minutes + marinating time | Cooking Time: 8 hours | Serves: 12

Ingredients

8 lb crown pork roast, trimmed

Salt and pepper to taste

10 garlic cloves, minced

4 tbsp honey Dijon mustard

2 tbsp apple cider vinegar

2 tbsp dark brown sugar

A handful of fresh sage

Gravy ingredients

1 cup butter

6 cloves garlic, minced

¼ cup flour

½ cup white wine

⅓ cup chicken broth

Salt and black pepper to taste

Directions

Preheat your smoker to 225°F. Place the rack in the lowest position. Fill the water pan with the wood chips. Season the pork with salt and pepper. Rest it for 1 hour at room temperature.

In a bowl, combine the garlic, Dijon honey mustard, apple cider vinegar, and sugar. Brush the mixture well over the pork. Adjust the digital thermometer inside any meat part.

Place the crown pork roast in the electric smoker. Cook until the temperate reading is 180-200°F. Remove the pork from the smoker and preheat the gas grill. Finish it over the grill flames for a more texture outer layer.

Meanwhile, prepare the gravy by heating butter in a large skillet over medium heat. Add the dripping from the pan inside the smoker. Add the broth and bring the mixture to a boil.

Afterward, reduce the heat and let it simmer. Add salt, pepper, garlic, flour, and white wine. Place the crown roast on a plate and drizzle gravy on top.

Chili Pork Shoulder

Prep Time: 40 minutes + marinating time | Cooking Time: 12 hours | Serves: 6

Ingredients

6 lb pork shoulder, Boston butt

Brine ingredients

½ cup molasses   10 oz pickling salt

Rub ingredients

2 tsp ground cumin   2 tbsp chili powder
1 tsp ground fennel   2 tbsp onion powder
1 tsp coriander   ½ tbsp paprika

Directions

Combine molasses, pickling salt, and 6-8 cups of water in a large bowl to make brine. Put the pork into the brine for about 8 hours. Then, remove and pat it dry. Apply all the rub ingredients evenly all over the pork.

Preheat your electric smoker to 225°F. Add the wood chips to the smoker. Place the meat on the sheet pan and transfer it to the top mostrack of the smoker. Insert a probe thermometer for heat measurements inside the meat. Smoke for12 hours. Once the internal temperature reaches 190°F, the meat is done. Let the pork rest for 20 to 30 minutes before serving.

Mustard Smoked Pork

Prep Time: 40 minutes + marinating time | Cooking Time: 4 hours | Serves: 4-6

Ingredients

4 lb pork shoulder

½ cup yellow mustard

4 tbsp Worcestershire sauce

2 tbsp smoked paprika

3 tbsp lemon pepper

2 tbsp cayenne pepper

1 tbsp garlic powder

Salt and black pepper to taste

⅓ cup apple cider vinegar

1 cup apple juice

Directions

Whisk the mustard, Worcestershire sauce, paprika, lemon pepper, cayenne pepper, garlic powder, salt, and black pepper in a bowl. Spread the mixture all over the pork and then wrap the shoulder with a plastic wrap. Place it in the refrigerator to marinate for 12 hours.

Preheat your smoker to 220°F. Remove the pork shoulder from the fridge. Combine apple cider vinegar, ½ cup of water and apple juice in a spray bottle. Soak smoking chips in water in a bucket by the smoker. Place the handful of smoking chips into the smoking basket.

Place the marinated pork in the smoker. Spray it with bottle liquid every 45-60 minutes. Cook for about 4 hours. Let it sit for 1 hour before serving.

Hawaiian Pork Rolls

Prep Time: 40 minutes | Cooking Time: 2-3 hours | Serves: 5

Ingredients

2 (4 lb) pork tenderloins

Cooking spray

16 sweet Hawaiian rolls

Sauce ingredients

2 cups ketchup

½ cup dark brown sugar

4 tbsp apple cider vinegar

2 tbsp Worcestershire sauce

2 tsp BBQ sauce

Salt and black pepper to taste

½ tsp garlic powder

½ chopped onion

2 tbsp apple juice

Rub ingredients

Kosher salt to taste

2 tsp garlic pepper seasoning

Directions

Preheat your electric smoker to 225°F. Preheat a saucepan on a smoking rack. Add the sauce ingredients and cook for 5-6 minutes. Remove and let the sauce cool.

Now in a separate bowl, mix the dry rub ingredients. Take the tenderloins, fold the thin edges, and tie them with a string. Season the tenderloins with the rub. Spritz the tenderloins with cooking spray.

Place the pork tenderloins on the middle rack of the smoker. Smoke until the thermometer reads 165°F of internal temperature, about 2-3 hours. Remove the pork from the heat and allow resting for 5 minutes. Slice the tenderloin and place it between toasted buns or rolls. Drizzle with prepared sauce and serve.

Whiskey & Cherry Glazed Ham

Prep Time: 40 minutes | Cooking Time: 2-3 hours | Serves: 3

Ingredients

2 lb spiral cut ham
Kosher salt and black pepper to taste

2 tbsp canola oil
5 oz cherry juice

Glaze ingredients

1 cup cherry preserves
⅓ cup light brown sugar, packed
⅓ cup maple syrup
½ cup water
1 oz honey whiskey
2 tbsp Dijon mustard

1 tsp cinnamon
½ tsp Cayenne pepper
1 tsp ground cloves
½ tsp garlic powder
2 tbsp butter

Directions

Combine all the glaze ingredients in a pot, and let it cook for a few minutes until sugar dissolved. Then set aside for further use. Add more water if the consistency is too thick.

Preheat your smoker to 225°F. Combine the cherry juice with 1 tablespoon canola oil in a separate bowl and set aside. Drizzle the remaining canola oil over the ham and rub well. Season the meat with salt and pepper. Cook in the smoker for 2-3 hours.

Keep basting the ham after every 30 minutes with the prepared basting mixture. When the internal temperature reaches 165°F, the ham is ready. Let it sit at room temperature for 10 minutes. Brush a final layer of basting mixture. Serve with the prepared sauce.

Garlic-Herb Rack of Pork

Prep Time: 60 minutes + marinating time | Cook Time: 3 hours | Serves 8

Ingredients

4 garlic cloves, finely chopped
2 shallots, finely chopped
1 cup panko bread crumbs
2 tbsp fresh oregano, chopped
2 tbsp fresh sage, chopped
1 tbsp fresh rosemary, chopped

½ tsp nutmeg
3 tbsp Dijon mustard
Salt and ground black pepper to taste
3 tbsp extra-virgin olive oil
1 (8-rib) bone-in pork loin, excess fat trimmed
2 lemons, cut into wedges

Directions

In a bowl, mix garlic, shallots, bread crumbs, oregano, sage, rosemary, nutmeg, mustard, salt, and pepper. Gradually add the olive oil and mix everything until it forms a paste. Rub the paste all over the pork loin. Wrap it tightly in plastic wrap and refrigerate for 12 hours or overnight.

Preheat your electric smoker to 225°F by adding mild or wood chips. Remove the pork from the refrigerator and put it on a smoking tray in the middle of the smoker.

Smoke for 2-3 hours until the meat reaches an internal temperature of 165°F. Pull the pork loin out of the heat and loosely cover it with foil. Let it sit for 15-20 minutes. Serve sliced with lemon.

Pork Loin with Pistachios

Prep Time: 40 minutes | Cooking Time: 5 hours | Serves: 6

Ingredients

5 lb pork loin, trimmed
2 tbsp canola oil
3 tbsp garlic powder
2 tbsp dried rosemary, chopped

Salt to taste
½ cup dry pistachios, chopped and roasted
2 tbsp ground black peppercorns

Directions

Load the electric smoker with apple wood chips and preheat it to 225°F. Brush the pork with canola oil. Now, rub all the listed spices over the pork and then let the pork rest for 10 minutes.

Preheat your electric smoker to 225°F. Insert the probe thermometer for heat measurements inside the meat. Smoke for 3-5 hours until the internal temperature reaches 200°F. When the pork is done, take it out and let it sit for a few minutes before serving.

Sweet Pork Steaks with Beer

Prep Time: 40 minutes + marinating time | Cooking Time: 2 hours | Serves: 4

Ingredients

4 pork shoulder steaks

1 cup BBQ sauce

1 cup beer

Rub ingredients

1 tsp paprika

Salt and black pepper to taste

1 tbsp brown sugar

2 tsp garlic powder

2 tsp onion powder

Directions

Preheat your electric smoker to 225°F by adding apple wood chips. Combine all the rub ingredients in a bowl. Rub the steaks with the mixture and then refrigerate for 30 minutes.

Combine the beer and BBQ sauce in a small bowl. Brush the steak with BBQ sauce mix and place inside the smoker for cooking for about 45 minutes. After 10 minutes of cooking, brush the pork steak with more BBQ sauce to keep it moist. Cook for 45 minutes at 325°F.

Once the internal temperature reaches 185°F, the steak is ready to be served. Take the steak out of the electric smoker and then serve with more BBQ sauce if liked.

Whiskey Teriyaki Pork Meatloaf

Prep Time: 40 minutes | Cooking Time: 6 hours | Serves: 4

Ingredients

2 lb ground pork

Salt and black pepper to taste

4 garlic cloves, minced

2 tsp light soy sauce

2 tbsp lemon juice

1 tbsp brown sugar

½ tsp cayenne pepper

½ cup pineapple juice

½ cup teriyaki sauce

2 tbsp Jack Daniels whiskey

Directions

Season the pork with salt and pepper and mix well with your hands. Form a meatloaf and poke it with a fork. Combine the remaining ingredients and brush the resulting glaze all over the meatloaf. Cook the meatloaf in your electric smoker for 6 hours at 225°F. Baste the meat with the remaining glaze every 30 minutes. Let it sit for 20 minutes before serving.

POULTRY RECIPES

Mexican-Style Beer-Brined Chicken Wings

Prep Time: 40 minutes + marinating time | Cook Time: 2 hours | Serves 6

Ingredients

3 limes, thinly sliced

3 limes, quartered lengthwise, for serving

¼ cup salt

¼ cup wildflower honey

1 tsp dark brown sugar

1 jalapeño pepper, thinly sliced

2 tbsp fresh rosemary, chopped

3 fresh bay leaves

3 (12-oz) bottles Corona beer

6 lb bone-in skin-on chicken wings

Salt and ground black pepper to taste

Directions

Mix the lime slices, salt, honey, sugar, jalapeño pepper, rosemary, bay leaves, and beer in a bowl. Put the chicken wings and the marinade in a large ziplock bag. Seal the bag and gently shake to combine. Put the bag in the fridge and leave it for 4-6 hours, shaking the bag occasionally.

Preheat your electric smoker to 275°F by adding hickory smoker chips. Remove the bag from the fridge, drain the marinade, and pat dry the wings. Arrange them on a smoking tray.

Season with salt and pepper. Place the tray into the electric smoker and cook for 2 hours or until the wings' temperature reaches 165°F. Serve with limes and enjoy.

Creole Chicken Gumbo

Prep Time: 40 minutes | Cook Time: about 4 hours | Serves 6

Ingredients

2 tbsp olive oil

2 shallots, chopped

1 ½ cups long-grain white rice

1 tbsp fresh thyme, chopped

3 cups chicken stock

½ cup canola oil

3 lb chicken thighs

1 tbsp Creole seasoning

8 oz andouille sausage, thinly sliced

6 thick-cut smoked bacon slices

1 cup flour

6 garlic cloves, minced

1 diced yellow onion

1 chopped celery stalk

1 green bell pepper, diced

1 quart vegetable stock

12 okra, cut into ½-inch slices

6 tomatoes, diced

3 bay leaves

Crusty bread for serving

Directions

Warm the olive oil in a saucepan over medium heat. Sauté the shallots for 6-8 minutes until golden brown. Sprinkle with salt and pepper. Stir in the rice, thyme, and bay leaf for 1-2 minutes. Pour in the chicken stock cook for 15-20 minutes until the stock is absorbed.

Now, preheat your electric smoker to 280°F. Add the cherry wood chips and let the smoke release. Season the chicken with Creole seasoning and place it on smoking trays, skin-side up. Smoke for about 2 hours until the internal temperature reaches 165 F.

Pour the canola oil into a deep roasting pan. Add the andouille sausage and bacon and insert them into the smoker. Cook for 40-45 minutes, turning the pan 2-3 times. Stir in the flour for 30 seconds and add the garlic, onion, celery, and green pepper.

Cook for about 20 minutes until tender. Pour in the vegetable stock to deglaze the pan, scraping up any browned bits from the bottom. Add the okra, tomatoes, thyme, and bay leaves. Stir to combine. Once the chicken is cooked, add it to the casserole on top of the other ingredients.

Smoke for 50-60 minutes or until the liquid reaches your desired consistency. Remove the chicken from the gumbo, pull the meat from the bones, and shred it with a fork. Return it to the gumbo, taste it, and adjust the seasoning. Serve with rice and crusty bread.

Chili Balsamic Chicken with Basil

Prep Time: 40 minutes + marinating time | Cooking Time: 2 hours | Serves: 4

Ingredients

4 tbsp olive oil

½ cup balsamic vinegar

4 cloves garlic, minced

2 tbsp basil, fresh

1 tsp red chili powder

Salt and black pepper to taste

2 lb chicken breasts, boneless and skinless

Directions

Take a zipper-lock plastic bag and combine all the ingredients except chicken. Place the chicken in the bag and let it marinate in the refrigerators for 2 hours.

Preheat your electric smoker to 250°F and add cherry or apple wood chips to the smoker. Place the chicken into the smoker once the smoke starts to come out. Cook until the internal temperature reaches 165°F. Use the digital meat thermometer to measure the temperature.

Peppery Chicken Cacciatore

Prep Time: 40 minutes | Cook Time: about 4 hours | Serves 4

Ingredients

2 whole chickens, separated into breasts, thighs, legs, and wings

2 tbsp flour

Salt and black pepper to taste

2 tbsp butter

1 yellow onion, thinly sliced

1 green bell pepper, thinly sliced

1 red bell pepper, thinly sliced

2 celery stalks, sliced

12 white mushrooms, quartered

8 garlic cloves, very thinly sliced

2 tbsp tomato paste

1 cup white wine

4 Roma tomatoes, diced

2 rosemary sprigs, finely chopped

1 tsp dry oregano

1 bay leaf

1 cup vegetable stock

1 tsp red chili flakes

Directions

Preheat your smoker to 280°F. Add cherry or applewood chip. Mix the flour, salt, and pepper in a bowl and add the chicken pieces. Toss to coat, shaking off any excess. Arrange the chicken pieces on smoking trays. Cook for 2 hours or until the internal temperature reaches 170°F.

Melt the butter in a large casserole over medium heat. Add the onion, bell peppers, celery, mushrooms, and garlic and gently stir for 3-5 minutes. Sprinkle with salt and pepper. Stir in the tomato paste. Place the casserole on a smoking tray and cook in the smoker for about 1 hour until the vegetables are tender.

Pour the white wine to deglaze the casserole, scraping off any browned bits. Add the tomatoes, rosemary, oregano, bay leaf, and vegetable stock and gently stir to combine. Arrange the smoked chicken pieces all over the vegetables and place back the casserole in the smoker. Cook uncovered for 1 hour until tender. Top with chili flakes and serve warm.

Herby Spatchcock Chicken

Prep Time: 40 minutes | Cook Time: about 3 hours | Serves 4

Ingredients

2 whole chickens

2 tbsp olive oil

8 garlic cloves, minced

2 tbsp smoked paprika

2 tbsp ground coriander

1 lime, zested

¼ cup ground ancho chile pepper

2 tbsp thyme, chopped

2 oregano, chopped

Salt and black pepper to taste

Directions

On a work surface, lay a chicken breast facing down and cut along the backbone with a sharp knife, starting at the tail end and working your way up to the neck.

Pull apart the two sides, opening up the chicken. Turn it over, breast-side up, pressing down with your hands to flatten the bird. Transfer to a greased baking dish. Repeat.

Load your electric smoker with the wood chips, then preheat it to 250°F. Whisk together the olive oil, garlic, smoked paprika, coriander, lime zest, chile pepper, thyme, oregano, salt, and pepper in a bowl.

Gently massage the spice mixture onto the chickens on all sides. Place them, skin-side down, on a smoking rack. Smoke for 3 hours or until the internal temperature reaches 170°F and juices run clear. Enjoy!

Asian-Inspired Chicken Drumsticks

Prep Time: 40 minutes + marinating time | Cook Time: 2 hours | Serves 4

Ingredients

2 lb chicken drumsticks

8 garlic cloves, peeled

3 tbsp sliced, peeled fresh ginger

2 tbsp cilantro, chopped

1 seeded Thai chile pepper, halved

¼ cup rice vinegar

2 tbsp fish sauce

2 tbsp tamari sauce

2 tbsp paprika

Salt and black pepper to taste

Directions

Place the garlic, ginger, cilantro, Thai chile pepper, rice vinegar, fish sauce, tamari sauce, and paprika in a food processor and blend until smooth. Remove the mixture to a large zipper bag. Add the chicken, seal, and shake to coat. Marinate in the fridge for 24 hours, turning 2-3 times.

The next day, arrange the wood chips in the electric smoker and then preheat it to 250°F. Remove the chicken, keeping the marinade in the refrigerator. Sprinkle the drumsticks with salt and pepper and arrange them on smoking trays. Smoke for 25-30 minutes.

Remove the marinade from the fridge and brush the drumsticks with it. Smoke for another 60-90 minutes, basting occasionally with the marinade until the chicken reaches an internal temperature of 165°F. Remove and let the chicken sit covered for 10 minutes.

Jamaican-Style Chicken

Prep Time: 40 minutes | Cook Time: 3 hours | Serves 4

Ingredients

2 whole chickens
Salt and ground black pepper to taste
1 garlic bulb, halved
8 thyme sprigs

8 rosemary sprigs
2 oranges, quartered and seeded
2 tbsp butter, softened
½ cup honey

Jamaican Rub

2 tbsp dark brown sugar
2 tbsp Jamaican seasoning
1 tbsp garlic powder
1 tbsp onion powder
1 tsp ground ginger
1 tbsp ground cinnamon

1 tsp smoked paprika
1 tsp ground cayenne pepper
1 tsp ground cloves
1 tsp ground nutmeg
Salt and ground black pepper to taste

Directions

Preheat your smoker to 275°F by adding apple wood chips. Salt and pepper the chickens. Fill each chicken cavity with ½ head of garlic, 4 thyme sprigs, 4 rosemary sprigs, and 4 orange pieces. Tuck in the wings and truss the drumsticks together with kitchen twine.

Place the Jamaican rub ingredients in a medium bowl and stir to incorporate well. Brush the chickens with butter and then generously rub them with Jamaican spice.

Place the chickens on smoking trays and drizzle them with half of the honey. Cook for 2-3 hours or until internal temperature registers 165°F in the thigh. Remove the chickens and cover them with foil. Let them rest for 10 minutes before drizzling with the remaining honey.

Sriracha Chicken Skewers

Prep Time: 40 minutes + marinating time | Cook Time: 2 hours | Serves 4

Ingredients

½ cup lemon juice
½ cup olive oil
2 tbsp thyme, finely chopped
2 tbsp sriracha sauce
2 tbsp tomato paste

1 crushed garlic clove
1 tbsp dark brown sugar
2 chicken breasts, cut into bite-size pieces
Salt and black pepper to taste

Directions

Blend the lemon juice, olive oil, thyme, lime slices, sriracha sauce, tomato paste, garlic, brown sugar, salt, and pepper in a large bowl. Add the chicken and toss to coat. Place the bowl covered with plastic wrap in the fridge for 12-24 hours, turning the chicken 2-3 times.

Preheat your smoker to 250°F. Add the cherry wood chips and let the smoker release smoke. Remove the chicken, reserving the marinade in the fridge. Thread the chicken onto 8 skewers.

Arrange the skewers on smoking trays and smoke them for 25-30 minutes. Brush the chicken with the reserved marinade and cook for another 25-30 minutes or until the internal temperature reaches 165°F.

Old-Fashioned Chicken Marbella

Prep Time: 40 minutes + marinating time | Cook Time: 4 hours | Serves 6

Ingredients

2 (3-lb) chickens, whole, separated into breasts, legs, thighs, and wings

¼ cup olive oil	3 bay leaves
½ cup red wine vinegar	Salt and ground black pepper to taste
6 garlic cloves, minced	1 cup white wine
¼ cup fresh oregano, chopped	½ cup muscovado sugar
1 cup dried pitted prunes	¼ cup parsley, chopped
½ cup capers	1 lemon, zested
½ cup pitted Spanish green olives	

Directions

Whisk together the olive oil, vinegar, garlic, and oregano in a bowl. Add the prunes, capers, olives, bay leaves, and chicken pieces. Toss to coat and cover with cling film. Place in the fridge for 20-24 hours, turning the chicken 2-3 times.

Preheat your electric smoker to 275°F. Add cherry or applewood chip to the smoker. Remove the chicken and pat it dry. Place the marinade in the fridge. Sprinkle the chicken with salt and pepper and transfer it to smoking trays, skin-side up. Smoke for about 2 hours or until the internal temperature reaches 165°F.

Mix the white wine and reserved marinade into a roasting pan. Add the cooked chicken and cover it with muscovado sugar. Insert the pan into the smoker and cook for 1-1 ½ hours, brushing it periodically until the sauce has reduced by half. Sprinkle with parsley and lemon zest and pour the prune and olive pan sauce over. Remove and discard the bay leaves; serve.

Maple-Glazed Chicken

Prep Time: 40 minutes | Cook Time: about 2 hours | Serves 4

Ingredients

4 boneless skinless chicken breasts
2 tbsp olive oil
1 tsp garlic powder
Salt and ground black pepper to taste

2 limes, juiced and zested
8 lime wedges
1 tsp dry lemon thyme
¼ cup maple syrup

Directions

Preheat your electric smoker to 280°F. Add the cherry wood chips to the smoker and let the smoke release. Drizzle the chicken with olive oil and season with garlic powder, salt, pepper, lime zest, and lemon thyme. Arrange the chicken, breast-side up, on smoking trays.

Smoke for about 2 hours until the internal temperature reaches 170°F. Pour the lime juice over the chicken and drizzle with the maple syrup. Smoke for another 15 minutes. Garnish with lime wedges, squeeze them over and serve.

Dijon Chicken Sandwiches

Prep Time: 30 minutes + marinating time | Cook Time: about 1 hour | Serves 4

Ingredients

4 boneless skinless chicken breasts
2 cups milk
2 tsp milk lemon juice
2 tbsp white wine vinegar
1 tbsp Dijon mustard
1 tbsp honey

Salt and black pepper to taste
6 tbsp extra-virgin olive oil
2 cups Iceberg lettuce, torn
1 cup finely sliced white onion
1 tbsp tarragon, chopped
4 buns, halved

Directions

Mix the milk and lemon juice in a large bowl. Add the chicken and stir to combine well. Cover the bowl with plastic wrap and place in the refrigerator for at least 12 hours.

Preheat your electric smoker to 275°F by adding mild or wood chips. Remove the chicken and pat it dry with paper towels. Whisk the vinegar, Dijon mustard, honey, salt, and pepper in a large bowl. Gradually pour in olive oil while whisking further. Add the lettuce, white onion, and tarragon. Set aside.

Arrange the chicken breasts on smoking trays. Smoke for 55-60 minutes. Cover the cooked chicken loosely with foil and leave to rest for 8-10 minutes. Using a sharp knife, slice the chicken thinly across the grain. Assemble the sandwiches by putting the chicken on the bottom bun and topping with lettuce salad.

Smoked Cajun Whole Chicken

Prep Time: 40 minutes | Cooking Time: 4 hours | Serves: 5

Ingredients

1 (5-lb) whole chicken

½ cup Cajun seasoning

Directions

Turn the chicken breast side down. Cut along the spine, and remove the backbone from the chicken. Press the breast bit down so the chickens get flat. Rub the chicken with the Cajun spice mix.

Place the chicken on a rack. Place the thermometer into the chicken. Place it in the electric smoker. Fill the wood chips holder with cherry or apple wood chips. Fill the water container with water. Close the door and set the temperature to 250°F. Cook until temperature reaches 165°F, 4 hours. Serve.

Ginger-Garlic Chicken Breasts

Prep Time: 40 minutes + marinating time | Cooking Time: 90 minutes | Serves: 2

Ingredients

2 chicken breasts
4 cloves minced garlic
2-inches ginger, minced
4 lemons, juiced

4 tbsp olive oil
Salt and black pepper to taste
1 tsp turmeric

Directions

Combine salt, pepper, lemon juice, olive oil, turmeric, ginger, and garlic in a bowl. Mix well and rub the chicken with the prepared mix. Marinate for 2 hours in the fridge.

Preheat your electric smoker to 250°F. Add the cherry wood chips to the smoker and let the smoke release. Place the chicken into the smoker. Cook for 90 minutes or until the internal temperature reaches 165°F.

Skillet Thyme Chicken with Grapes

Prep Time: 40 minutes | Cook Time: 2 hours | Serves 4

Ingredients

2 tbsp olive oil

2 tbsp unsalted butter

8 chicken thighs

Salt and black pepper to taste

4 thyme sprigs

1 cup seedless green grapes

1 cup seedless red grapes

¼ cup honey

¼ tbsp balsamic vinegar

2 cups sauvignon blanc wine

1 cup vegetable stock

Directions

Preheat your smoker to 250°F and add cherry wood chips. Preheat a large cast-iron skillet by placing it on a smoking rack, then add the olive oil and butter. Season the chicken thighs with salt and pepper. Place them in the skillet among the grapes and top with thyme sprigs.

Smoke for 55-60 minutes until a meat thermometer reads an internal temperature of 160°F. Drizzle the chicken with honey. Pour the balsamic vinegar, white wine, and vegetable stock into the skillet. Put the skillet back into the smoker. Continue smoking for 25-30 minutes until desired consistency is achieved. To serve, spoon the sauce over the chicken and enjoy!

White Wine Chicken with Dumplings

Prep Time: 40 minutes | Cook Time: about 3 hours | Serves 4

Ingredients

1 (3-4-lb) chicken, cut into parts (breasts, thighs, legs, and wings)

Salt and ground black pepper to taste

1 tbsp olive oil

1 lb smoked bacon slices, cut into strips

2 diced carrots

2 diced celery stalks

4 diced green onions

8 garlic cloves, thinly sliced

1 tbsp fresh thyme, chopped

2 cups sauvignon blanc wine

2 quarts hot water

3 bay leaves

4 cups all-purpose flour

1 tbsp baking soda

1 tsp baking powder

1 cup sour cream

5 tbsp butter, melted

3 tbsp fresh thyme, chopped

Directions

Preheat your electric smoker to 275°F by adding mild or wood chips. Mix 1 cup of flour with salt and pepper to taste. Roll the chicken pieces in the flour, then shake off the excess. Place them on smoking trays. Adjust the target temperature to 165°F.

Pour the olive oil into a large cast-iron pot and put it on a smoking rack to preheat it. Add bacon and stir to coat with the oil. Smoke for 30 minutes. Mix in the carrots, celery, green onions, garlic, and thyme and season with salt and pepper. Smoke for about 1 hour.

Deglaze the pot by pouring the white wine and scraping off the bottom to eliminate any browned beef bits. Pour in 8 cups of hot water and bay leaves. Add the smoked chicken pieces and put them back into the smoker. Smoke for about 1 hour.

Remove the skin and bones from the chicken pieces and discard them. Roughly shred the chicken using two forks. Return the shredded meat to the pan. Discard the bay leaves.

Whisk the remaining flour, baking soda, baking powder, salt, and pepper in a bowl. Add the sour cream, melted butter, and thyme. Shape the dough into small balls. Add them to the pot, then return the pot to the smoker for 25-30 minutes until the dumplings are cooked through.

Chicken Thighs with Scallions

Prep Time: 40 minutes + marinating time | Cooking Time: 90 minutes | Serves: 2

Ingredients

2 lb chicken thighs

6 tbsp soy sauce

3 tsp sesame oil

4 garlic cloves

4 scallions

1 tbsp thyme

1 tsp allspice

⅓ tsp cinnamon

⅓ tsp crushed red pepper

Directions

Combine soy sauce and oil in a bowl and rub it gently over the chicken thighs. In a food processor, blend together garlic, scallion, thyme, cinnamon, allspice, and red pepper. Blend it until smooth. Rub it all over the thighs and seal the chick in the zip-lock plastic bag. Let it marinate for about 2 hours.

Preheat your electric smoker to 250°F by adding the cherry wood to the smoker. Smoke the chicken for 90 minutes. Adjust the thermometer to read the internal temperate. Once the internal temperature reaches 165°F, remove the chicken. Let it sit for 10 minutes, then serve.

Agave Glazed Whole Chicken

Prep Time: 40 minutes + marinating time | Cooking Time: 2 hours | Serves: 3

Ingredients

2 lb whole chicken

2 tbsp melted butter

1 cup grapefruit juice

2 cups chicken stock

Rub ingredients

Black pepper and salt to taste

4 garlic cloves, minced

2 tsp onion powder

2 tsp ginger, minced

1 tsp five-spice powder

Glaze ingredients

4 tsp coconut milk

2 tbsp sesame oil

4 tbsp agave syrup

2 tbsp lemon juice

2 tbsp melted butter

Directions

Prepare the glaze by heating the coconut milk in a small pot over medium heat. Add sesame oil, agave syrup, lemon juice, and butter. Cook for 5-6 minutes and reserve for further use.

Pour the chicken stock and grapefruit juice into a large pot over medium heat. Bring to a boil and turn off the heat. Submerge the chicken and let it sit for 2 hours.

After, combine all the rub ingredients in a bowl. Take the chicken out of the liquid, pat it dry with kitchen paper, and then rub it with the prepared rub mixture.

Preheat your smoker to 250°F. Add cherry or apple wood chips. Place the chicken in the smoker. Cook for about 2 hours, basting it with the agave glaze every 30 minutes. When ready, let it rest for 10 minutes. Pour the remaining glaze and butter and serve.

Lemon Chicken with Herbs

Prep Time: 40 minutes + marinating time | Cooking Time: 90 minutes | Serves: 2-3

Ingredients

15 cups filtered water

4 cups nonalcoholic beer

3 tbsp salt

1 cup brown sugar

1 tbsp rosemary

1 tsp sage

2 lb whole chicken, giblets removed

4 tbsp butter

| 3 tbsp olive oil | 2 tbsp garlic powder |
| 1 cup Italian seasoning | Zest of 3 small lemons |

Directions

Add the filtered water, salt, and brown sugar to a large pot over medium heat. Bring to a boil and stir until the salt and sugar dissolve. Add the herbs and cook for 5 minutes until aromatic. Pour in the beer and then immerse the chicken in it. Let it refrigerate for 3 hours.

Remove the chicken from the brine, and then pat dry with a paper towel. Uncover and let it sit for one more hour at room temperate. Next, butter the chicken. Massage the chicken for fine coating. Next, rub the chicken with Italian seasoning, garlic powder, and lemon zest.

Load electric smoker with the wood chips, and preheat to 250°F until smoke starts to build. Then, slow roast it for 1.5-hours, and keep basting with olive oil every 30 minutes. Once the internal temperature reaches 165°F and the juices run clear. Serve and enjoy!

Curry Chicken Legs with Spicy Orange Glaze

Prep Time: 40 minutes + marinating time | Cooking Time: 2 hours | Serves: 5

Ingredients

| 15 chicken legs | 6 tbsp butter, melted |

Rub ingredients

4 tsp sugar	½ tsp ground ginger
⅓ tsp kosher salt	¼ tsp garlic powder
¼ tsp black pepper	¼ tsp tiger seasoning
⅓ tsp curry powder	½ tsp cinnamon, powder

Glaze ingredients

| 1 cup orange marmalade | 2 tbsp Sriracha sauce |
| 6 tbsp chicken stock | 2 tbsp rice wine vinegar |

Directions

Preheat your smoker to 250°F. Combine all the rub ingredients in a bowl. Rub the chicken with the rub and coat it with melted butter. Place the chicken on the upper rack of your electric smoker and let it cook for 45 minutes. Turn the rack every 10 minutes.

Mix the glaze ingredients in a small saucepan over medium heat. Stir and cook for 5 minutes. Turn the heat off, then strain the sauce. After 25 minutes of cooking, baste the legs with the glaze. Cook for 35 more minutes. Serve and enjoy.

Tangy Chicken with Carrots

Prep Time: 40 minutes | Cooking Time: 5 hours | Serves: 6

Ingredients

3 lb whole chicken, giblets removed

2 tbsp dried oregano

2 tbsp dried thyme

1 tbsp dried rosemary

1 tsp smoked paprika

Salt and black pepper to taste

2 tsp garlic powder

3 tsp lemon pepper

2 carrots, diced

2 celery stalks, diced

2 onions, diced

4 tbsp dill weed

2 tbsp olive oil

Directions

Preheat your electric smoker to 250°F. In a small bowl, combine the thyme, oregano, paprika, rosemary, salt, black pepper, lemon pepper, and garlic powder. Brush the chicken with olive oil, then generously rub it with the spice mix. Tie the legs together using kitchen string. For a nice presentation, fold the wings back and under the back.

Transfer the chicken to the smoking rack. Place the diced vegetables in a cast-iron skillet and insert them into the smoker. Smoke for 5 hours. Once the internal temperate of the chicken reaches 165°F, the dish is ready. Just before 20 minutes remain, add the dill weeds. Using a fork, shred the chicken into pieces. Mix it with the juices. Serve with the vegetables.

BBQ Marinated Chicken Breasts

Prep Time: 40 minutes + marinating time | Cooking Time: 90 minutes | Serves: 2

Ingredients

2 lb of chicken breasts, split

4 tsp barbecue rub

8 tbsp melted butter

Salt and black pepper to taste

Directions

Combine BBQ rub and melted butter in a bowl and let it cool at room temperature. Take a marinade injector and inject the prepared rub into the chicken breasts.

Prepare your smoker by preheating it to 250°F and adding apple wood chips. Place the breasts into the smoker. Use a digital probe thermometer to read the internal temperature to 165°F. Once it reads 165°F, serve.

African-Style Smoked Whole Chicken

Prep Time: 40 minutes + marinating time | Cooking Time: 3 hours | Serves: 3

Ingredients

1 (3.5-lb) whole chicken

Spice ingredients

1 tsp fresh cilantro

4 tbsp olive oil

1 tsp garlic powder

1 tbsp onion powder

1 tsp cumin

1 tsp paprika

½ tsp ground red pepper

1 tbsp dry lemon zest

Salt, to taste

Directions

Preheat your electric smoker to 250°F by adding cherry wood chips. Tie the legs of the chicken together using a kitchen string. Combine all the spice ingredients in a small bowl and rub the spice blend onto the chicken. Place it on a baking rack and put it inside the smoker. Cook until internal temperate reaches 165°F, about 3 hours. Take out the chicken and let it sit for 15 minutes before serving.

Sriracha Chicken Wings

Prep Time: 40 minutes | Cooking Time: 2 hours | Serves: 2

Ingredients

2 lb chicken wings

2 tsp garlic powder

Sea salt and black pepper to taste

2 tsp fresh cilantro leaves, minced

Sauce ingredients

⅓ cup raw honey

⅓ cup Sriracha sauce

2 tbsp coconut amino

3 limes, juiced

Directions

Combine all the sauce ingredients in a separate bowl and set aside. Season the chicken with garlic, salt, and pepper. Preheat your electric smoker to 250°F. Add cherry or apple wood chips to the smoker. Place the chicken into the smoker once the smoke starts to come out. Close the door and cook for about 2 hours. Cook until the internal temperature reaches 165°F. Use the digital meat thermometer to measure the temperature. Serve.

Buffalo Chicken Balls with Ranch Dipping

Prep Time: 40 minutes + marinating time | Cooking Time: 90 minutes | Serves: 4

Ingredients

2 lb ground chicken

3 tbsp cooked carrot, finely chopped

4 tbsp celery, finely chopped

2 green onions, finely chopped

⅓ cup dry bread crumbs

⅓ tsp salt

⅓ tsp paprika

⅓ tsp brown sugar

⅓ tsp garlic powder

⅓ tsp ground black pepper

Ranch dip ingredients

⅓ cup non-fat Greek yogurt

⅓ cup mayonnaise

2 tbsp buttermilk

⅓ tsp seasoned salt

¼ tsp dill

½ tsp chili powder

¼ tsp granulated garlic

Buffalo sauce ingredients

½ cup hot sauce

⅓ cup butter

⅓ tsp Worcestershire sauce

Directions

Combine celery, carrots, chicken, onions, bread crumbs, and salt, sugar, garlic, paprika, and pepper in a bowl. Mix well to form the meatballs. Freeze at least for 30 minutes. Combine the entire ranch dip ingredient in a bowl. Refrigerate for 20 minutes.

Preheat your smoker to 250°F. Place the buffalo sauce ingredients in a pot over medium flame. Simmer for 10 minutes. Arrange the meatballs on a pan sheet and place them on the topmost rack. Cook for about 40 minutes, turning them once. Once the internal temperature reaches 165°F, remove the meatballs and pour the buffalo sauce over them. Return to the smoker and cook for 50 more minutes. Serve with ranch dip.

Honey Chicken Wings

Prep Time: 40 minutes + marinating time | Cooking Time: 2 hours | Serves: 4

Ingredients

⅓ cup rice vinegar

3 tbsp honey

½ cup soy sauce

⅓ cup sesame oil

2 tbsp garlic sauce

1 tbsp garlic salt, to taste

16 chicken thighs, skinless, boneless

Directions

Combine rice vinegar, honey, soy sauce, sesame oil, chili garlic sauce and salt in a bowl, then coat chicken thighs with the mixture. Refrigerate for 6 hours.

Preheat your electric smoker to 255°F. Add cherry wood chips to the smoker. Place the marinated chicken into the smoker. Cook for 2 hours.

Smoked Paprika Chicken Quarters

Prep Time: 40 minutes | Cooking Time: 2 hours | Serves: 3

Ingredients

2 tsp brown sugar

⅓ cup maple syrup

⅓ cup Sriracha sauce

Salt and black pepper to taste

⅓ tsp smoked paprika

3 lb chicken meat

Directions

Add 2 cups of water, brown sugar, Sriracha sauce, salt, pepper, paprika, and maple syrup to a large pan over a low flame. Cook for 5 minutes or until the sugar dissolves. Remove from the heat and let it get cool off. Reserve this sauce for later use.

Set your electric smoker to 250°F. Cook the chicken in it for 2 hours. Remember to baste the chicken with the prepared sauce every 20 minutes with a brush. Once the digital thermometer meets 165°F, serve with the reserve dripping and remaining sauce.

Easy BBQ Chicken Wings

Prep Time: 40 minutes + marinating time | Cooking Time: 2 hours | Serves: 4

Ingredients

2 lb chicken wings

1 cup BBQ sauce

Directions

Cut the chicken wings and discard the tips. Marinate the wings in the BBQ sauce for about 2 hours. Preheat your electric smoker to 250°F. Add the cherry wood chips to the smoker and let the smoker release smoke. Place the chicken into the smoker. Cook for 2 hours.

Smoked Turkey Poblano Poppers

Prep Time: 40 minutes | Cook Time: about 4 hours | Serves 8

Ingredients

2 tbsp extra-virgin olive oil

1 diced white onion

2 garlic cloves, minced

Salt and ground black pepper to taste

2 cups long-grain white rice

1 tbsp fresh thyme, chopped

1 fresh bay leaf

4 cups vegetable stock

2 andouille sausages, casings removed and sliced

2 plum tomatoes, diced

2 scallions, sliced diagonally

2 cups shredded cheddar cheese

8 poblano peppers, halved lengthwise

2 (4-lb) fresh bone-in skin-on turkey breasts

2 tbsp chopped fresh cilantro

Directions

Warm the olive oil in a saucepan over medium heat. Sauté the onion and garlic for 3-5 minutes until softened. Stir in the rice, thyme, and bay leaf for 1-2 minutes. Pour in the vegetable stock and stir gently. Bring to a boil and lower the heat. Simmer for 45-60 minutes until the liquid is absorbed. Discard the bay leaf.

Preheat your electric smoker to 275°F. Add wood chips to begin the smoke. Arrange the stuffed peppers on the smoking rack in an even layer. Set aside. Rub the turkey breasts with salt and pepper. Place them on a baking pan and then cook inside the smoker for 4 hours or until golden brown and until the internal temperature reaches 165°F.

Shred the turkey, discarding any bones. Mix together the sausage, tomatoes, scallions, shredded turkey, and rice in a bowl. Divide the mixture between the poblano pepper halves. Top the stuffed peppers with cheddar cheese and place them under the broiler for 4 minutes on high until the cheese is completely melted. Garnish with fresh cilantro. Serve and enjoy!

Middle Eastern Turkey Soup

Prep Time: 60 minutes | Cook Time: about 3 hours | Serves 4

Ingredients

2 tbsp olive oil

2 turkey thighs

1 cup diced green beans

1 diced carrot

1 diced celery stalk

1 diced yellow onion

4 garlic cloves, minced

Salt and black pepper to taste

32 oz vegetable stock

4 Yukon gold potatoes, peeled and diced

1 cup diced tomatoes

2 tbsp fresh basil, chopped

3 bay leaves

1 cup bulgur wheat

2 tbsp grated Parmesan cheese

Directions

Preheat your electric smoker to 250°F by adding mild or wood chips. Preheat a large cast-iron saucepan by placing it on a smoking rack, then pour in the olive oil. Place the turkey thighs on smoking trays. Add the green beans, carrot, celery, onion, and garlic to the saucepan and sprinkle with salt and pepper.

Let's smoke for 1 hour. Deglaze the saucepan by pouring in the vegetable stock and 8 cups of hot water, scraping off any browned bits from the bottom. Next, add the potatoes, tomatoes, basil, and bay leaves. Smoke for a further 2 hours. After 1 hour, stir in the bulgur wheat and add the turkey thighs.

Continue to smoke for the remaining 1 hour. When ended, remove the thighs, remove the bones, and discard them. Shred the meat with 2 forks and add it back to the soup. Remove and discard the bay leaves. Serve the soup in bowls scattered with Parmesan cheese.

Turkey Goujons with Sweet Chili Sauce

Prep Time: 40 minutes | Cook Time: about 1 hour | Serves 4

Ingredients

2 tbsp smoked paprika

2 tbsp dried mustard

1 tbsp ground ancho chile pepper

Salt and black pepper to taste

2 cups all-purpose flour

3 eggs, lightly beaten

4 cups panko bread crumbs

1 boneless skinless turkey breast, cut into strips

1 cup sweet chili sauce

Directions

Preheat your smoker to 275°F with mild or any other apple or cherry wood chips. Blend the paprika, dried mustard, ancho pepper, salt, pepper, and flour in a shallow bowl. Beat the eggs lightly in another shallow bowl, and pour the bread crumbs into a third large bowl.

Roll the turkey strips in the flour mixture, submerge them into the eggs, and lastly the bread crumbs. Arrange them on baking sheets, leaving enough room between each strip. Smoke the turkey goujons for 50-60 minutes until golden brown. Remove to a serving platter. Serve with sweet chili sauce for dipping.

Caribbean Sausage Stuffed Turkey

Prep Time: 60 minutes + marinating time | Cook Time: 5 hours | Serves 6

Ingredients

1 cup brown sugar

2 cups sea salt

¼ cup rainbow peppercorns

1 tbsp whole allspice berries

12 unpeeled garlic cloves, smashed

2 lime, thinly sliced

4 fresh bay leaves

6 rosemary sprigs

6 thyme sprigs

6 cilantro sprigs

1 (12-lb) whole turkey

Salt and black pepper to taste

1 loaf sourdough bread, cubed

½ cup breadcrumbs

1 quart vegetable stock

2 tbsp olive oil

6 oz butter, softened

2 diced celery stalks

1 diced onion

1 leek, thinly sliced

½ tsp chili powder

1 tbsp fresh thyme, chopped

1 tbsp fresh rosemary, chopped

1 tbsp fresh sage, chopped

Directions

Pour 2 gallons of water into a large pot over high heat. Add the brown sugar, sea salt, rainbow peppercorns, allspice berries, garlic, lime, bay leaves, rosemary, thyme, and cilantro and bring the ingredients to a boil. Decrease the heat and simmer for 5 minutes, stirring often to incorporate all the ingredients. Turn off the heat and leave the brine to cool completely. Submerge the turkey into the brine, cover, and refrigerate overnight.

Warm the olive oil in a skillet over medium heat. Sauté the sausage until browned, 10 minutes; set aside. Add and melt half of the butter in the skillet. Stir in the celery, onion, leek, chili powder, thyme, rosemary, and sage for 3-5 minutes, then pour in the vegetable stock. Cook for about 15 minutes. Turn off the heat, add the breadcrumbs and sausage, and stir the mixture well. Set aside.

The next day, remove the turkey from the brine and, using kitchen paper, pat the turkey dry. Salt and pepper the turkey cavity. Fill it with the stuffing and secure the skin underneath with cocktail sticks. Using kitchen twine, tie the legs together.

Preheat your electric smoker to 275°F. Add the cherry wood chips and let the smoker release smoke. Rub the remaining softened butter over the turkey and season with salt and pepper. Place the stuffed turkey on a smoking rack and insert it into the smoker. Smoke for about 4 hours or until internal temperature registers 165°F on an instant-read thermometer.

Remove the turkey to a serving platter and cover it with foil. Let it rest for at least 20 minutes before carving. Serve and enjoy!

Turkey Tacos with Kimchi Slaw

Prep Time: 40 minutes + marinating time | Cook Time: 2 hours | Serves 4

Ingredients

½ tsp Gochujang powder
1 cup cilantro, chopped
3 garlic cloves, minced
1 chili pepper, diced
¼ cup packed dark brown sugar
3 tbsp canola oil
3 tbsp soy sauce
1 tbsp toasted sesame oil
1 tsp ground coriander
1 (4-6-lb) bone-in skin-on turkey breast

Salt and black pepper to taste
1 red onion, very thinly sliced
1 cup rice vinegar
4 cups shredded Napa cabbage
4 scallions, thinly sliced
1 carrot, thinly sliced
1 cup fresh cilantro leaves
12 large flour tortillas, warm
2 peeled avocados, sliced

Directions

Place the Gochujang powder, cilantro, garlic, chili pepper, sugar, canola oil, soy sauce, sesame oil, coriander, and pepper in a bowl. Whisk until well combined. Add the turkey and toss to combine. Place in the fridge covered for at least 4 hours, flipping the turkey occasionally.

Preheat your electric smoker to 275°F by adding hickory smoker chips. Remove the turkey, reserving the marinade in the fridge. Sprinkle the turkey with salt and pepper and place it on a baking tray.

Smoke the turkey for about 2 hours. The internal temperature of the turkey should be around 170°F once done the cooking. Remove the turkey from the smoker, cover it with aluminum foil, and let it sit for a few minutes. Then, thinly slice the turkey across the grain.

Combine the red onion and rice vinegar in a small saucepan and insert it into the smoker. Cook for 30 minutes until the onion is tender. Place the cabbage, scallions, carrot, and cilantro in a salad bowl. Season with salt and pepper. Add the warm pickled red onion with the liquid. Toss to coat.

Remove the reserved marinade from the fridge and pour it into a small saucepan over medium heat. Simmer for 14-16 minutes until the liquid is reduced to 2/3. Divide the slaw, avocado, and turkey between the tortillas and drizzle with the marinade sauce. Serve.

Paprika Turkey with Chimichurri Sauce

Prep Time: 40 minutes + marinating time | Cooking Time: 4 hours | Serves: 5

Ingredients

5 lb bone-in turkey pieces
Salt and black pepper to taste
1 tsp paprika
½ tsp cayenne
2 tbsp olive oil

1 pepper
1 onion
2 carrots, chopped
2 scallions
2 tomatoes, chopped

Chimichurri Sauce

½ cup olive oil
1 tsp parsley
1 tsp red pepper flakes

2 garlic cloves
2 red onions

Directions

Arrange the wood chips in your electric smoker and preheat it to 230°F. Season the turkey with salt, pepper, paprika, and cayenne pepper. Transfer the turkey to the sheet pan and arrange peppers, onions, carrots, scallion, and tomatoes beside it. Drizzle with olive oil.

Place the pan sheet in the smoker. Cook for 4 hours. Check the turkey to an internal temperature of 165°F. To make the chimichurri, blend all the homemade chimichurri ingredients in a blender and puree until combined. Serve the turkey and veggies with sauce.

Morocco-Style Turkey

Prep Time: 40 minutes + marinating time | Cooking Time: 4 hours 20 minutes Serves: 5

Ingredients

5 lb turkey, trimmed
1 cup olive oil
5 tbsp Ras el Hanout

Kosher salt, to taste
Zest of 3 lemons
2 tbsp chopped mint leaves

Directions

Cut the turkey's backbone, remove the spine, and discard the fat. Flip the turkey breast-side up and hand-press into the breastbone to flatten it. Rub the turkey with oil and then massage the seasoning with salt and lemon zest. Cover the turkey with plastic wrap and marinate it for 30 minutes.

Preheat your smoker to 250°F. Soak the wood chips in water one hour before smoking. Remove plastic wrap and cook the turkey for 4 hours 20 minutes. Garnish it with mint.

Smoked Turkey with Green Beans

Prep Time: 40 minutes | Cooking Time: 2 hours | Serves: 4

Ingredients

2 lb fresh green beans

4 cups chicken stock

1 lb turkey meat, sliced

3 tbsp apple cider vinegar

Salt and black pepper to taste

Directions

Add wood chips to the smoker and preheat your electric smoker to 220°F. Place the green beans and 1 cup of water in a microwave-safe container. Microwave for 4 minutes. Drain the water. Pat dry the beans with a paper towel. Transfer the beans to a pan and add the chicken stock and turkey.

Set the temperature to 250°F. Cook for 2 hours. Once done, drain the excess liquid. Sprinkle with salt, pepper, and a drizzle of apple cider vinegar. Serve and enjoy!

Buttered Turkey with Apple

Prep Time: 40 minutes | Cooking Time: 10 hours | Serves: 10

Ingredients

1 (10 lb) whole turkey

4 cloves garlic, crushed

½ cup butter

1 (12-oz) cola-flavored carbonated beverage

1 apple, quartered

1 onion, quartered

1 tbsp garlic powder

1 tbsp salt

1 tbsp black pepper

Directions

Preheat your electric smoker to 225°F. Rub the turkey with seasoned salt. Place it in a roasting pan. Combine cola, butter, apples, garlic powder, salt, and pepper in a bowl.

Fill the cavity of the turkey with the resulting mixture. Rub the butter and crushed garlic outside of the turkey as well. Cover the turkey with foil. Smoke the turkey for 10 hours at 250°F. Once it's done, serve.

Bourbon Turkey

Prep Time: 40 minutes + marinating time | Cooking Time: 10 hours | Serves: 14

Ingredients

½ cup salt

⅓ cup molasses

⅓ cup granulated sugar

½ cup Worcestershire sauce

6 garlic cloves, minced

4 dried bay leaves

Black pepper to taste

14 lb whole turkey

2 cups bourbon

1 cup canola oil for coating

Directions

Pour a gallon of water, salt, sugar, molasses, garlic, Worcestershire sauce, bourbon, pepper, and bay leaves into a large pot. Boil it for a few minutes and then cool it completely. Submerge the turkey completely in the brine using a large bucket. Brine it in the liquid for 15 hours.

Preheat your electric smoker to 250°F and load it with soaked wood chips. Take the turkey out of the brine and pat it dry with paper towels. Rub the turkey with oil and place the turkey in the smoker. Cook for 10 hours until the internal temperate is 165°F. Serve.

Juicy Herbed Turkey

Prep Time: 40 minutes | Cooking Time: 12 hours | Serves: 16

Ingredients

16 lb turkey

2 tbsp dried thyme

1 tbsp dried sage

2 tsp dried oregano

2 tsp paprika

1 tbsp sea salt

Black pepper, to taste

1 tsp dried rosemary

Zest of 1 orange

⅓ cup extra-virgin olive oil

⅓ cup apple cider

⅓ cups water

Directions

Preheat your electric smoker to 250°F. Take a small bowl and mix all the dry spices and ingredients. Rub it gently over the rekey meat. In the end, drizzle olive oil on top.

Pour water and apple cider into the large water pan at the bottom of the electric smoker. Place a drip pan on the next rack or shelf of the smoker. Fill the sides with the apple wood chips.

Place the turkey on the top rack of the smoker. Close the door of the rack and then cook for approximately 12 hours. Add more wood if smoke stops coming. Use the digital probe thermometer to get an internal temperature of 165°F. Remove the turkey and serve.

Duck Breast with Marsala-Cherry Sauce

Prep Time: 40 minutes | Cook Time: about 2 hours | Serves 4

Ingredients

1 tbsp canola oil

4 duck breasts

Salt and ground black pepper to taste

4 rosemary sprigs

1 yellow onion, diced

1 cup vegetable stock

12 fresh cherries, halved and pitted

½ cup Marsala wine

2 tbsp butter

2 tbsp parsley, chopped

Directions

Preheat your electric smoker to 275°F and load the smoker with soaked wood chips. Preheat a cast-iron dish by putting it on a smoking rack and pouring in the canola oil. Put the duck breasts on a chopping board, skin side up.

Use a sharp knife to score a ½-inch criss-cross pattern in the duck fat, being careful not to cut through to the flesh. Salt and pepper the breasts and top them with rosemary sprigs.

Arrange them on smoking trays. Add the onion to the cast-iron dish, stirring gently to coat in the oil, and sprinkle with salt and pepper. Smoke for about 30 minutes. Deglaze the dish by pouring in the vegetable stock and scraping off any browned bits from the bottom.

Finally, add the cherries. Smoke for another 90 minutes. When the internal temperature has reached 135°F, remove the duck from the smoker. Move it to a serving platter and leave it to rest for 10-15 minutes.

Keep cooking the onion for 8-10 more minutes until the cooking juice in the pan is almost evaporated. Pour in the Marsala wine and continue to cook until the desired consistency of the sauce is reached.

Stir in the pot and cook until the sauce is reduced to your desired consistency. Finish the sauce by adding the butter and swirling it in the dish until butter is incorporated.

Cut the duck breasts into thin slices and pour the cherry sauce over the top and serve garnished with fresh parsley.

Peking-Style Duck with Clementines

Prep Time: 40 minutes | Cook Time: 4 hours | Serves 4

Ingredients

2 tbsp canola oil

1 duck, whole

Salt and black pepper to taste

4 clementines, halved

8 thyme sprigs

8 shallots, halved

8 blue plums, halved and pitted

4-star anise, whole

4 cloves, whole

2 cinnamon sticks, whole

3 cups Riesling wine

4 green onions, sliced diagonally

Directions

Preheat your electric smoker to 275°F. Add the cherry wood chips to the smoker and let the smoke release. Brush a roasting pan with canola oil; set aside. Sprinkle the duck all over with salt and pepper. Place 4 clementine halves and 4 thyme sprigs in the duck cavity.

Transfer the stuffed duck breast-side up to the roasting pan. Arrange the shallots, plums, star anise, cloves, cinnamon sticks, remaining clementine halves, and remaining thyme sprigs around the duck. Cover with white wine and sprinkle with salt and pepper.

Cook in the smoker for about 2 hours, spooning the rendered liquids over the entire dish periodically. Continue smoking for another 1-2 hours, or until the internal temperature reaches 165°F. Take out the duck of the smoker, loosely cover it with aluminum foil, and let it sit for 15-20 minutes. Discard the thyme, star anise, and cinnamon sticks. Sprinkle with green onions.

Turmeric Smoked Duck

Prep Time: 40 minutes | Cooking Time: 90 minutes | Serves: 4

Ingredients

1 tsp dry coriander

Salt and black pepper to taste

1 tsp turmeric

1 lb boneless and skinless duck breast, sliced

Directions

Preheat your electric smoker to 225°F and load the smoker with soaked wood chips. Toss the duck with coriander, salt, pepper, and turmeric in a large bowl. Smoke the duck for 90 minutes or until the internal temperature reaches 165°F. Once done, remove it from the heat. Let stand, loosely covered with aluminium foil, for 10 minutes. Serve.

FISH AND SEAFOOD

Rosemary Salmon Wrapped in Bacon

Prep Time: 40 minutes | Cook Time: about 1 hour | Serves 4

Ingredients

2 tbsp unsalted butter

4 (8-oz) Chinook salmon fillets, trimmed

2 tbsp rosemary tarragon, minced

1 tsp garlic powder

1 tsp chili powder

Salt and ground black pepper to taste

12 bacon slices

3 lemons, halved

Directions

Preheat your electric smoker to 275°F by adding apple wood chips. Preheat a cast-iron skillet by placing it on a smoking rack. Add the butter and olive oil to warm up.

In a small bowl, mix together tarragon, garlic powder, chili powder, salt, and pepper and rub the mixture onto both sides of the salmon fillets. Wrap each salmon fillet with 3 bacon strips and roll them in the skillet to coat with the butter. Then, put them on a smoking rack and smoke for 35-45 minutes or until the bacon is brown and crispy. Serve with lemons.

Honey-Almond Crusted Salmon

Prep Time: 40 minutes | Cook Time: about 30 minutes | Serves 4

Ingredients

4 trimmed salmon fillets, skin removed

2 lemons, juiced and zested

½ tsp chipotle powder

1 tsp smoked paprika

Salt and ground black pepper to taste

1 lemon, cut into wedges

1 cup almonds, finely chopped

1 cup honey

Directions

Preheat your electric smoker to 275°F and add wood chips. In a small bowl, mix lemon zest, chipotle, paprika, salt, and pepper and rub the mixture onto both sides of the salmon fillets.

Transfer the fillets to a maple plank and drizzle them with honey. Press the chopped almonds over. Top with lemon juice and put the plank on a smoking rack. Smoke for about 30 minutes until the salmon is crisp and lightly browned. Serve with lemon wedges.

Alaskan Salmon & Asparagus Scrambled Eggs

Prep Time: 40 minutes | Cook Time: about 30 minutes | Serves 4

Ingredients

1 lb Alaskan salmon, cut into strips

Salt and ground black pepper to taste

2 tbsp unsalted butter

1 lemon, juiced

8 large eggs, lightly beaten

1 cup heavy cream

2 chopped green onions

2 asparagus, chopped

8 crusty artisan bread 8 slices

¼ cup Greek yogurt, whipped

Directions

Preheat your electric smoker to 275°F and add wood chips. Season the salmon fillets with salt and pepper and put them on the smoking racks. Drizzle with lemon juice and smoke for 25-30 minutes, or until the salmon turns opaque.

Preheat a cast-iron skillet by placing it on a smoking rack, then add the butter. Mix the eggs, heavy cream, green onions, asparagus, salt, and pepper in a large bowl. Pour the egg mixture into the skillet and smoke until the egg whites have set and the yolks are still runny, stirring often.

Take out the skillet from the heat while stirring. Arrange the bread slices on smoking racks and smoke them for about 5 minutes, or until toasted. Divide the scrambled eggs between the toasted bread. Top with salmon. Garnish with a dollop of yogurt and serve.

Dijon Roasted Salmon

Prep Time: 40 minutes | Cook Time: about 30 minutes | Serves 4

Ingredients

2 tbsp Dijon mustard

¼ cup mayonnaise

2 tbsp dill, finely sliced

1 lemon, juiced and zested

1 tsp ground fennel seeds

1 tsp ground coriander

1 tsp garlic powder

Salt and ground black pepper to taste

1 lemon, cut into wedges

4 salmon fillets, skin removed

Directions

Preheat your electric smoker to 275°F and add wood chips. In a large bowl, whisk together the Dijon mustard, mayonnaise, ground fennel seeds, coriander, lemon zest, half of the lemon juice, garlic powder, salt, and pepper. Spread the mayonnaise mixture on the salmon fillets.

Transfer them to smoking racks. Drizzle with the remaining lemon juice and smoke for about 30 minutes until lightly browned. Top with dill and serve with lemon wedges.

Haddock with Tropical Tomato Salsa

Prep Time: 40 minutes | Cook Time: about 1 hour | Serves 4

Ingredients

4 haddock fillets

4 tbsp olive oil

Salt and ground black pepper to taste

2 cups diced pineapple

2 cups diced mango

2 tomatoes, seeded and chopped

1 red bell pepper, seeded, and diced

¼ cup diced red onion

1 chile pepper, trimmed, seeded, and diced

1 cup fresh cilantro, sliced

¼ tsp honey

1 lime, juiced and zested

Directions

Preheat your electric smoker to 275°F by adding apple wood chips. In a large bowl, combine the pineapple, mango, tomatoes, red bell pepper, onion, chile pepper, and cilantro.

Whisk the honey, lime zest, lime juice, salt, and pepper in a small bowl and add to the pineapple mixture. Stir to combine and place in the refrigerator until ready to use.

Coat the haddock fillets with 2 tbsp olive oil, salt, and pepper. Put them on smoking racks and smoke for 10-15 minutes or until the fish is opaque. When ready, remove the haddock from the heat to a serving platter and top with the salsa. Drizzle with the remaining olive oil.

Easy Smoked Salmon

Prep Time: 40 minutes | Cooking Time: 2 hours | Serves: 2

Ingredients

2 lb salmon fillets

4 tbsp melted butter

2 tbsp lemon juice

Salt and black pepper to taste

Directions

Preheat your electric smoker to 225°F. Add wood chips to begin the smoke. Now brush the butter over the fillets. Pour lemon juice over the fillets. Sprinkle a generous amount of pepper and salt to taste. Place salmon into the electric smoker. Cook for 2 hours. Once the fillets temperature reaches 150°Fahrenheit, it's done. Serve and enjoy.

Fast Sole Meunière

Prep Time: 40 minutes | Cook Time: about 30 minutes | Serves 2

Ingredients

3 tbsp unsalted butter

2 lemon sole fillets, skin removed

½ cup all-purpose flour

Salt and ground black pepper to taste

1 lemon, zested and juiced

2 tbsp chopped parsley

2 tbsp capers

1 lemon, cut into wedges

Directions

Preheat your electric smoker to 275°F by adding apple wood chips. Preheat a large cast-iron skillet by placing it on a smoking rack and adding the butter to melt and brown. Season the sole fillets with salt and pepper, then roll them in the flour, dusting off the excess.

Carefully put the fillets in the browned butter and sprinkle with lemon zest. Smoke for 25-30 minutes, flipping them halfway through cooking. Once the time is done, remove the fillets from the heat. Drizzle them with browned butter. Top with parsley and capers. Serve with lemon.

Halibut with Mixed Mushrooms

Prep Time: 40 minutes | Cook Time: about 1 hour | Serves 4

Ingredients

2 tbsp unsalted butter

2 tbsp olive oil

4 Alaskan halibut fillets, skin removed

Salt and ground black pepper to taste

8 oyster shiitakes mushrooms, torn lengthwise

4 chanterelle mushrooms, torn lengthwise

4 crimini mushrooms, sliced lengthwise

4 garlic cloves, diced

2 tbsp thyme, finely diced

2 lemons, cut into wedges

2 tbsp parsley, chopped

Directions

Preheat your smoker to 275°F by adding apple wood chips. Coat the halibut with olive oil, salt, and pepper. Smoke it on smoking racks for 10-15 minutes or until the flesh is opaque.

Preheat a cast-iron skillet by placing it on a smoking rack, then add the butter to melt. Stir in mushrooms, garlic, thyme, salt, and pepper. Smoke for 25-30 minutes, tossing them gently.

When the fish is ready, remove it from the heat, and allow it to rest for about 5 minutes. Top the halibut with mushrooms and parsley. Serve with lemon wedges on the side.

Tilapia Curry with Naan

Prep Time: 40 minutes | Cook Time: about 1 hour | Serves 4

Ingredients

½ tsp Kashmiri chili powder

½ tsp ground turmeric

1 tsp ground cumin

¼ tsp ground cinnamon

¼ tsp ground cloves

¼ tsp ground nutmeg

¼ cup coconut oil

½ tsp fennel seeds, whole

1 tbsp coriander seeds, whole

4 cardamom pods

4 garlic cloves, finely chopped

2 tbsp finely grated fresh ginger

1 cinnamon stick, whole

12 fresh curry leaves

1 red onion, sliced

2 tomatoes, cut into thin wedges

2 red chile peppers, halved lengthwise

2 lemongrass stalks, cut into rounds

2 lb tilapia fillets, skin removed

Salt and ground black pepper to taste

1 cup coconut milk

1 tbsp fresh cilantro, chopped

Directions

Preheat your electric smoker to 275°F by adding apple wood chips. Whisk the Kashmiri chili powder, turmeric, cumin, ground cinnamon, cloves, and nutmeg in a small bowl and set aside.

Preheat a large cast-iron skillet by placing it on a smoking rack, then pour in the coconut oil. Place the fennel, coriander, cardamom pods, garlic, ginger, and cinnamon stick in a pestle and blend the mixture into a paste.

Move the paste to the skillet and smoke for 20 minutes, gently stirring periodically. Add the curry leaves, red onion, tomatoes, chile peppers, lemongrass, salt, and pepper and smoke for 20 minutes.

Sprinkle tilapia fillets with the previously prepared spice mix on all sides. Gently place them on smoking racks. Smoke for 10-15 minutes or until the tilapia flesh is opaque.

Deglaze the skillet by pouring 1 cup of water and scraping up any brown bits from the bottom. Add the coconut milk and smoke for 15-20 minutes or until the desired consistency of the sauce is reached. Adjust the seasoning with salt and pepper, add the tilapia fillets and cilantro and serve.

Silky Tilapia Ceviche

Prep Time: 40 minutes | Cook Time: 1 hour + cooling time | Serves 4

Ingredients

2 lb tilapia fillets, skinned and diced

Salt and ground black pepper to taste

½ cup finely diced red onion

2 limes, juiced and zested

1 lime, cut into wedges

3 tbsp cilantro, finely sliced

1 tbsp finely grated fresh ginger

1 jalapeño pepper, finely sliced

Tortilla chips, for serving

Directions

Preheat your electric smoker to 225°F and add wood chips. Season the tilapia fillets with salt and pepper on both sides. Put them on smoking racks. Smoke for 1 hour until the tilapia flesh is opaque. Place the onion, zest, lime juice, cilantro, ginger, and jalapeño in a bowl.

When the time is over, remove the tilapia from the heat and leave it to cool slightly, then flake it with. a fork. Transfer the flaked fish to the onion mixture; gently mix to combine. Macerate in the refrigerator for 2 hours. Spoon the ceviche into a bowl. Serve with tortilla chips.

Lemon Cod with Olives & Capers

Prep Time: 40 minutes | Cook Time: about 1 hour | Serves 2

Ingredients

2 tbsp unsalted butter

1 tsp oil, divided

2 cod fillets, trimmed

¼ tsp shallot powder

1 lemon, grated and juiced

Salt and ground black pepper to taste

2 cups white wine

1 cup mixed olives, pitted and halved

1 tbsp capers

1 cayenne chile pepper, sliced

1 tbsp parsley, finely chopped

Directions

Preheat your electric smoker to 275°F by adding apple wood chips. Preheat a large cast-iron skillet by placing it on a smoking rack, then add the butter. Rub the cod fillets with lemon zest, shallot powder, salt, and pepper on all sides and transfer them to the skillet, flesh-side down.

Smoke for 14-16 minutes until golden brown, then remove them from the skillet. Put the fillets flesh-side up on a smoking rack above the skillet.

Deglaze the saucepan by pouring the white wine and scraping up any browned bits from the bottom. Stir in the olives, capers, olive oil, chile pepper, salt, and pepper.

Smoke the cod and the pan sauce for another 14-16 minutes, then add the cod back to the skillet, flesh-side up. Continue smoking for 8-10 minutes until the fish flakes easily when pressed with a knife. Sprinkle with parsley. Serve drizzled with the sauce and lemon juice.

Savory Smoked Catfish Fillets

Prep Time: 40 minutes | Cooking Time: 5 hours | Serves: 5

Ingredients

5 catfish fillets

4 tbsp butter, soften

Rub ingredients

3 tbsp paprika

2 tbsp onion powder

½ tsp salt

⅓ tbsp dried thyme

2 tbsp garlic powder

⅓ tbsp cayenne powder

Directions

Mix all rub ingredients in a bowl. Lightly brush the fillets with butter. Sprinkle the generous amount of rub onto the fillets. Preheat the smoker to 225°F and add wood chips. Place the fish inside the smoker. Cook for 5 hours.

Thyme Smoked Eel with Lemons

Prep Time: 40 minutes + marinating time | Cooking Time: 3 hours | Serves: 2

Ingredients

2 eel fillets, cleaned and washed

Brine ingredients

10 cups warm water

4 lemons, halved

1 ½ cups salt

2 fresh thyme sprigs

½ cup brown sugar

Directions

First, prepare the brine by mixing all the brine ingredients in a large pot and placing the eel in it for 10 hours. Preheat your electric smoker to 235°F and add wood chips. Pat the eel dry. Smoke the eel for about 3 hours. Once the skins get crisp, the eel is ready to be served.

Crab Cakes with French Sauce

Prep Time: 40 minutes | Cook Time: about 1 hour | Serves 4

Ingredients

1 tbsp Dijon mustard

2 ¼ cups mayonnaise

1 cup dill pickles, diced

1 small onion, finely diced

2 tbsp capers, chopped

2 tbsp parsley, chopped

½ tsp dry tarragon

2 lemons, grated and juiced

Salt and ground black pepper to taste

4 tbsp olive oil

12 oz lump crabmeat

2 tbsp chives, finely sliced

1 large egg

½ cup bread crumbs

1 tsp Tabasco sauce

1 lemon, zested and juiced

1 lemon, cut into wedges

Directions

Place the mustard, 2 cups of mayonnaise, dill pickles, shallot, capers, parsley, tarragon, half of the lemon zest, half of the lemon juice, salt, and pepper and whisk well. Set aside.

Preheat your electric smoker to 275°F by adding apple wood chips. Preheat a large cast-iron skillet by placing it on a smoking rack, then pour in the olive oil.

Mix the crabmeat, remaining mayonnaise, chives, egg, bread crumbs, Tabasco sauce, lemon zest, lemon juice, salt, and pepper. Shape the meat mixture into 4 balls; flatten to make 6 patties.

Add the crab cakes to the skillet and smoke for about 40 minutes, turning them over halfway through cooking. Top with the French sauce and serve with lemon wedges on the side.

Cheddar Scallops with Mornay Sauce

Prep Time: 30 minutes | Cook Time: about 1 hour | Serves 4

Ingredients

8 sea scallops on the half shell, side muscle removed

2 tbsp unsalted butter

2 tbsp all-purpose flour

1 cup whole milk, cold

¼ tsp nutmeg

Salt and black pepper to taste

2 cups finely grated cheddar cheese

1 large egg yolk

2 tbsp cilantro, minced

2 lemons, quartered lengthwise

Directions

Prepare the mornay sauce by melting the butter in a saucepan over medium heat. Add the flour and whisk for 1-2 minutes, then gradually stir in the milk and cook until a thick, smooth sauce forms, 10 minutes.

Season with nutmeg, salt, and pepper and remove the saucepan from the heat. Stir in 1 cup of cheddar cheese and allow it to cool. Gently add the egg yolk and stir to combine.

Preheat your electric smoker to 275°F by adding apple wood chips. Top the scallops with the prepared Mornay sauce and place them on smoking racks Smoke for about 30 minutes until golden brown.

When ready, remove the scallops and scatter them with the remaining cheddar cheese and cilantro. Serve with lemon wedges.

Spanish Seafood Paella

Prep Time: 60 minutes | Cook Time: about 2 hours | Serves 8

Ingredients

3 tbsp olive oil

1 yellow onion, finely shredded

6 garlic cloves, minced

1 red bell pepper, diced

1 cup tomato sauce

2 cups bomba rice

4 cups fish stock

1 tsp ground turmeric

Salt and black pepper to taste

12 cleaned fresh mussels, beards removed

12 peeled fresh shrimp, deveined, tails left on

6 fresh squid, sliced

8 fresh clams, cleaned

1 cup green peas

2 lemons, cut into wedges

Directions

Preheat your electric smoker to 275°F by adding apple wood chips. Preheat a paella pan by placing it on a smoking rack, then pour in the olive oil. Place the

onion, garlic, and bell pepper. Smoke for 15-20 minutes until lightly browned. Stir in rice for 1-2 minutes, and then pour in the tomato sauce and fish stock, mixing gently. Sprinkle with turmeric, salt, and pepper and continue to smoke for 20 minutes.

Nestle the mussels, shrimp, squid, clams, and green peas into the rice. Smoke for about 1 hour or until the mussels and clams open and the squid and shrimp are opaque. Throw away any mussels or clams that did not open. Serve with lemon wedges.

Cajun-Style Garlic Shrimp

Prep Time: 40 minutes | Cook Time: about 30 minutes | Serves 4

Ingredients

2 tbsp butter

3 tbsp olive oil

1 baguette loaf, sliced

Salt and ground black pepper to taste

4 garlic cloves, finely sliced

1 tsp Cajun seasoning

¼ tsp red pepper flakes

2 lb shelled shrimp, deveined

1 lemon, juiced and zested

Directions

Preheat your electric smoker to 275°F and add cherry wood chips. Arrange the baguette slices on the smoking racks of the smoker. Drizzle them with 1 tbsp of olive oil and sprinkle them with salt and pepper. Preheat a cast-iron skillet by placing it on a smoking rack, then add the butter and the remaining olive oil.

Add the garlic, Cajun seasoning, red pepper flakes, salt, and pepper. Smoke for 15 minutes. Stir in shrimp and lemon zest. Smoke for about 30 minutes, turning the shrimp once until the flesh is slightly pink. Top the shrimp with lemon juice and serve with baguette slices.

French Mussels Mariniere

Prep Time: 40 minutes | Cook Time: about 30 minutes | Serves 2

Ingredients

1 yellow onion, finely diced

1 fennel bulb, thinly sliced

1 red chile pepper, very thinly sliced

4 garlic cloves, minced

1 tsp lemon zest

2 tbsp thyme, chopped

1 fresh bay leaf

3 tbsp butter

1 tbsp olive oil

Salt and ground black pepper to taste

1 baguette loaf, cut into slices

2 cups Chardonnay white wine

1 cup vegetable stock

3 lb mussels, cleaned

Directions

Preheat your smoker to 275°F by adding apple wood chips. Preheat a saucepan by placing it on a smoking rack. Place the butter to melt, then add the onion, fennel, red chile pepper, garlic, lemon zest, thyme, bay leaf, salt, and pepper. Smoke for 20 minutes, shaking from time to time.

Deglaze the saucepan by pouring in the white wine. Scrap up any browned bits from the bottom. Pour in the vegetable stock and stir. Sprinkle one side of the baguette slices with salt and pepper and drizzle them with olive oil. Place them on smoking racks, oiled-side up.

Smoke for about 10 minutes. Put the mussels in the saucepan and cover with a lid. Smoke for about 10 minutes until the mussels have all opened. Discard any that remain closed. Remove and discard the bay leaf before serving with the smoked bread. Enjoy!

Quick Smoked Trout

Prep Time: 40 minutes + marinating time | Cooking Time: 4 hours | Serves: 2

Ingredients

1 lb trout, pin bones removed

2 tbsp vegetable oil

1 cup dark-brown sugar

1 cup coarse salt

Directions

Make the brine by mixing 3 cups of water, brown sugar, and salt in a large pot. Submerge the fish in the brine for 10 hours. Then pat dry the fish and drizzle oil all over the trout.

Preheat your electric smoker to 225°F. Add the wood chips. Remove the fish from the brine and pat it dry with kitchen paper. Smoke the fish for 4 hours, then serve.

Sweet-Mustard Halibut

Prep Time: 40 minutes + marinating time | Cooking Time: 6 hours | Serves: 6

Ingredients

6 halibut fillets

1 cup honey mustard rub

⅓ cup kosher salt

1 cup brown sugar

1 tsp cumin

1 tbsp dried bay leaves, crushed

Directions

Add the kosher salt, brown sugar, cumin, bay leaves, and ½ gallon of water to a large bowl and stir well until the salt and sugar are dissolved. Insert the halibut and let it sit for 2 hours.

Preheat your electric smoker to 225°F and add the wood chips. Remove the fish from the brine and pat it dry with kitchen paper. Massage the halibut with the honey mustard rub.

Place the fish on a rack in the smoker. Cook for 6 hours or until the internal temperature of the fish reaches 150°F. Serve and enjoy.

Yakitori Prawn Skewers

Prep Time: 40 minutes + marinating time | Cook Time: 30 minutes | Serves 4

Ingredients

24 raw peeled prawns, deveined

1 pineapple, cubed

2 spring onions, chopped

4 garlic cloves, minced

4 scallions, finely sliced

¼ cup soy sauce

1 tbsp mirin

1 tsp sake

2 tbsp fish sauce

2 limes, juiced and zested

2 tbsp dark brown sugar

1 tbsp finely grated fresh ginger

1 tsp sesame oil

Salt and ground black pepper to taste

Directions

Whisk together the spring onions, garlic, scallions, soy sauce, mirin, sake, fish sauce, lime zest, lime juice, sugar, ginger, sesame oil, salt, and pepper in a large bowl. Pour the mixture into a large resealable bag, then add the prawns and pineapple cubes.

Remove as much air as possible from the bag before sealing it. Place the bag in the refrigerator for 3-4 hours, turning twice. Soak bamboo skewers in water for about 30 minutes.

Preheat your electric smoker to 275°F and add wood chips. Remove the prawns and pineapple, keeping the marinade in the refrigerator. Thread prawns and pineapple cubes onto the bamboo skewers. Transfer the skewers to smoking racks. Smoke for 10 minutes.

Drizzle the prawns and pineapple with the reserved marinade and smoke for another 15-20 minutes until the prawns are cooked and have turned pink. Serve and enjoy!

Smoked Tuna Steaks with Mayo-Garlic Dip

Prep Time: 40 minutes + marinating time | Cooking Time: 90 minutes | Serves: 2

Ingredients

2 lb tuna steaks

2 tbsp soy sauce

Brine ingredients

6-10 cups warm water

½ cup salt

Dip ingredients

½ cup mayonnaise

2 oz cream cheese

½ cup red onion, diced

⅓ cup fresh parsley, chopped

3 tbsp lemon juice

½ tbsp garlic powder

⅓ tsp black pepper

½ tbsp hot sauce

Directions

Prepare brine by combining the brine ingredients in a pot. Soak the tuna in the brine overnight. Afterward, rinse under tap water. Pat dry the tuna with a paper towel, then let it sit at room temperate to dry. Rinse, dry, and lightly coat with soy sauce.

Preheat your electric smoker to 250°F. Remove the tuna and pat it dry with paper towels. Place it on the smoking rack and smoke for about 90 minutes.

Make the sauce by mixing together the entire dip ingredient in a small bowl. Remove the tuna from the smoker and let it get cold. Chop the tuna if desired. Add chopped tuna to the dip and let it sit in a refrigerator for a few minutes. Then serve.

Tasty Smoked Fish with Celery Sauce

Prep Time: 40 minutes + marinating time | Cooking Time: 6 hours | Serves: 6

Ingredients

6 lb fish fillets

Brine ingredients

1 quart cold water

⅓ cup salt

1 cup brown sugar

½ cup soy sauce

½ cup vinegar

Sauce ingredients

½ cup almond milk

6 oz cream cheese, softened

⅓ cup finely minced onion

½ stalk celery, finely chopped

1 tbsp minced fresh parsley

½ tsp lemon juice

1 tsp Worcestershire sauce

Cayenne pepper, to taste

Salt and black pepper to taste

Directions

Combine the brine ingredients in a bowl and place the fish in the brine for 2 hours. Then, process the sauce ingredients in a blender until smooth paste forms.

Preheat your electric smoker to 250°F. Remove the fish and pat it dry with paper towels. Place it on the topmost rack of the smoker and cook for 6 hours. The internal temperature of fish should be about 150°F once done the cooking. Enjoy served with prepared sauce.

Drunken Manila Clams

Prep Time: 40 minutes | Cook Time: about 1 hour | Serves 4

Ingredients

1 onion, very thinly sliced

2 cilantro sprigs

2 fresh bay leaves ½ tsp nutmeg

1 cup water

1 cup vodka

10 peppercorns, whole

1 tbsp Worcestershire sauce

Salt and ground black pepper to taste

10 lb Manila clams, rinsed

Crusty bread to serve

Directions

Preheat your electric smoker to 275°F by adding apple wood chips. Preheat a cast-iron skillet by placing it on a smoking rack. Place the onion, cilantro, bay leaves, water, vodka, peppercorns, Worcestershire sauce, salt, and pepper in a large bowl and stir to combine. Pour the mixture into the pan.

Smoke for 18-20 minutes, stirring often. Then, add the clams to the pan, cover the pan with a lid, and continue smoking for 4-6 minutes until the clam shells have opened. Take off the lid and smoke the clams for another 2-3 minutes. Discard the unopened clams. Serve the clams with the sauce and crusty bread.

Maple Smoked Salmon

Prep Time: 40 minutes + marinating time | Cooking Time: 5 hours | Serves: 4

Ingredients

1 lb salmon

Brine ingredients

1 quart cold water

⅓ cup Diamond Crystal kosher salt

1 ½ cups maple syrup

1 cup brown sugar

Directions

Combine brine ingredients in a large bowl and place fish in for 2 hours. Next, pat the fish dry and put it on a rack. Smoke the fish at 225°F for 5 hours.

After one hour of cooking, baste the chicken with maple syrup and repeat every one hour. The internal temperature of fish should be about 150°F. Enjoy.

Smoked Salmon in Pineapple-Maple Glaze

Prep Time: 40 minutes + marinating time | Cooking Time: 6 hours | Serves: 6

Ingredients

6 lb fresh salmon

⅓ cup maple syrup

½ cup pineapple juice

Brine ingredients

⅓ cup sea salt (non-iodized)

1 cup pineapple juice

¼ cup brown sugar

3 tbsp Worcestershire sauce

2 tbsp garlic salt

Directions

Prepare the brine by mixing ½ gallon of water, pineapple juice, brown sugar, Worcestershire sauce, and garlic salt in a large pot. Submerge the fish in it for 2 hours.

Preheat your electric smoker to 225°F and add apple wood chips. Remove the fish from the brine and pat it dry with paper towels. Place the dry salmon in the smoker once the smoker starts to build. Cook it for 6 hours. Mix the pineapple juice with maple syrup and baste the fish every 30 minutes while cooking. Serve and enjoy!

Simple Brined Salmon

Prep Time: 40 minutes + marinating time | Cooking Time: 5 hours | Serves: 4

Ingredients

4 salmon fillets

¾ cup brown sugar

1 cup canning salt

½ tsp chili powder

½ tsp lemon pepper

1 cup white wine

Directions

Combine the sugar, salt, chili powder, lemon pepper, white wine, and 1 gallon of water in a pot and stir to dissolve the salt and sugar. Submerge the salmon and place the pot in the refrigerator for 2 hours or overnight.

Preheat the smoker to 225°F and add apple wood chips. Remove the salmon from the brine and pat it dry with paper towels. Place it on the smoking rack skin-side down. Smoke for 5 hours or until the fish reaches an internal temperature of 150°F. Try it-you'll love it!

VEGETABLES, SNACKS, AND SIDES

BBQ Baked Pinto Beans with Bacon

Prep Time: 40 minutes | Cook Time: about 2 hours | Serves 12

Ingredients

3 tbsp olive oil

1 lb bacon, cut into thin slices

1 yellow onion, diced

1 red bell pepper, diced

1 green bell pepper, diced

3 (14-oz) cans pinto beans

4 cups chicken stock

2 cups diced tomatoes

1 cup dark molasses

1 cup packed dark brown sugar

1 tbsp mustard powder

¼ tsp ground nutmeg

2 tbsp tomato paste

2 tbsp Worcestershire sauce

Salt and ground black pepper to taste

Directions

Preheat your smoker to 250°F by adding apple wood chips. Preheat a cast-iron casserole by placing it on a smoking rack, then pour in the olive oil. Place the bacon and smoke for 35-45 minutes, tossing often. Once done, add the onion, bell peppers, salt, and pepper and toss to coat. Smoke for another 30 minutes.

Blend the pinto beans, chicken stock, tomatoes, molasses, sugar, mustard powder, nutmeg, tomato paste, Worcestershire sauce, salt, and pepper in a bowl. Pour the bean mixture into the casserole and smoke for 1 ½ hours. When ready, remove the casserole from the heat.

Cheesy Cannellini Beans with Potatoes

Prep Time: 40 minutes | Cook Time: about 2 hours | Serves 8

Ingredients

2 tbsp olive oil

4 leeks, thinly sliced

8 Yukon Gold potatoes, sliced

1 garlic bulb, halved

Salt and ground black pepper to taste

1 cup white wine

1 cup vegetable stock

3 parsley sprigs, leaves stripped and minced

4 cups cannellini beans

1 lemon, grated and juiced

1 cup grated Parmigiano Reggiano cheese

Directions

Preheat your electric smoker to 275°F by adding apple wood chips. Preheat a cast-iron casserole by placing it on a smoking rack, then add the olive oil. Place the leeks, potatoes, and garlic halves, cut-side down, and season with salt and pepper. Smoke for 60 minutes.

Deglaze the saucepan by pouring in the white wine. Scrap up any browned bits from the bottom. Pour in the vegetable stock, parsley, beans, lemon zest, lemon juice, salt, and pepper.

Smoke for 50-60 minutes. Once done, remove the casserole from the heat, squeeze the garlic cloves from the head, and return them to the casserole. Top with Parmigiano cheese and serve.

Roasted Cauliflower with Pomodoro Sauce

Prep Time: 40 minutes | Cook Time: 2 hours | Serves 4

Ingredients

4 tbsp olive oil
1 garlic powder
1 leek, thinly sliced
½ tsp ground coriander
Salt and ground black pepper to taste
1 cup white wine
5 tomatoes, diced
1 cup vegetable stock
1 head cauliflower, cored

1 garlic bulb, halved
1 tsp smoked paprika
½ tsp dry oregano
1 lemon, zested
2 tbsp fresh basil, sliced
2 tbsp parsley, chopped
2 tbsp finely grated Parmesan cheese
2 tbsp flaked almonds, toasted

Directions

Preheat your electric smoker to 275°F by adding apple wood chips. Preheat a large cast-iron skillet by placing it on a smoking rack, then pour in 3 tbsp of the olive oil. Add the garlic powder, leek, ground coriander, salt, and pepper and toss to coat. Smoke for 15 minutes.

Deglaze the skillet by pouring in the white wine and scraping off any browned bits on the bottom. Pour in the tomatoes and vegetable stock. Coat the cauliflower and the garlic bulb with the remaining olive oil and place them on top of the tomatoes.

Sprinkle with salt and pepper and smoke for 60-90 minutes until tender. Remove the garlic and allow it to cool slightly. Once cool enough to handle, squeeze garlic cloves out of the garlic head and stir them into the sauce. Sprinkle with paprika, lemon zest, oregano, and basil. Slice the cauliflower into steaks and arrange the slice on a platter. Top with tomato sauce, Parmesan cheese, and almonds. Serve and enjoy!

Sticky Sweet Chili Carrots

Prep Time: 40 minutes | Cook Time: about 2 hours | Serves 8

Ingredients

2 tbsp unsalted butter

3 chili peppers, sliced

24 carrots, quartered lengthwise

3 tbsp thyme, chopped

¼ tsp light soy sauce

1 lime, zested

Salt and ground black pepper to taste

3 tbsp honey

Directions

Preheat your electric smoker to 250°F by adding apple wood chips. Preheat a large cast-iron skillet by placing it on a smoking rack. Then, add the butter to melt. Pour in the chili peppers, carrots, thyme, soy sauce, lime zest, salt, and pepper and stir.

Smoke for 55-60 minutes, turning once until the vegetables are sticky and glazed. When ready, remove the skillet from the heat. Discard the rosemary sprigs. Drizzle with honey and serve.

Homemade Maple Cornbread

Prep Time: 40 minutes | Cook Time: about 1 hour | Serves 8

Ingredients

1 ¼ cups flour

1 cup yellow cornmeal

½ cup granulated sugar

1 tbsp baking powder

1 tsp baking soda

½ tsp sea salt flakes

½ cup corn oil

1 cup milk

¼ cup maple syrup

3 tbsp butter, melted

2 large eggs, lightly beaten

1 cup corn kernels

Directions

Preheat your electric smoker to 275°F by adding apple wood chips. Blend together the flour, cornmeal, sugar, baking powder, baking soda, and salt in a medium bowl. Whisk together the milk, corn oil, maple syrup, melted butter, and eggs in a separate bowl until smooth.

Fold the wet ingredients into dry ingredients and gently stir to combine. Pour the batter into a greased skillet and smooth the top with a spatula. Top with corn kernels. Smoke for 50-60 minutes or until an inserted toothpick comes out clean. Remove from the heat and allow leaving in the pan for 2-3 minutes.

Hazelnut Asparagus

Prep Time: 40 minutes | Cook Time: 30 minutes | Serves 4

Ingredients

1 tbsp unsalted butter

1 tbsp olive oil

2 garlic cloves, thinly sliced

1 lb asparagus, trimmed

4 shallots, trimmed and quartered

Salt and ground black pepper to taste

1 lemon, halved and seeded

1 cup sliced hazelnuts

Directions

Preheat your electric smoker to 275°F by adding apple wood chips. Preheat a large cast-iron skillet by placing it on a smoking rack, then add the butter and olive oil. Stir in the garlic, asparagus, shallots, salt, and pepper. Add the lemon halves to the skillet, cut side down, and continue smoking for 10 more minutes. Top with hazelnuts and serve.

Authentic Basque Piperade

Prep Time: 40 minutes | Cook Time: about 2 hours | Serves 4

Ingredients

2 tbsp olive oil

4 garlic cloves, thinly sliced

2 shallots, finely diced

1 red bell pepper, julienned

1 yellow bell pepper, julienned

1 green bell pepper, julienned

½ tsp Spanish paprika

Salt and ground black pepper to taste

1 cup white wine

5 Roma tomatoes, quartered lengthwise

1 tsp sugar

5 black olives

2 tbsp basil leaves, thinly sliced

Directions

Preheat your electric smoker to 250°F by adding apple wood chips. Preheat a large cast-iron skillet by placing it on a smoking rack, then add the olive oil. Stir in the garlic, shallots, bell peppers, Spanish paprika, salt, and pepper. Smoke for 50-60 minutes. Deglaze the skillet by pouring in the white wine.

Scrap up any browned bits from the bottom. Add the tomatoes and sugar and continue smoking for another 25-30 minutes until slightly browned. Top with the basil and black olives. Serve and enjoy!

Shallot Fingerling Potatoes

Prep Time: 40 minutes | Cook Time: about 2 hours | Serves 8

Ingredients

2 lb fingerling potatoes, rinsed

4 tbsp duck fat

1 garlic clove, minced

8 shallots, quartered lengthwise

Salt and ground black pepper to taste

3 tbsp thyme, minced

Directions

Cook the potatoes in boiling salted water for about 15 minutes until tender. Drain, allow cooling slightly, then halve.

Preheat your smoker to 250°F by adding apple wood chips. Preheat a cast-iron skillet by placing it on a smoking rack, then add the duck fat to warm. Stir in the garlic, shallots, and potatoes and season with salt and pepper. Smoke the vegetables for about 1 hour, tossing occasionally. Garnish with thyme and serve.

Easy Root Vegetables

Prep Time: 40 minutes | Cook Time: about 2 hours | Serves 8

Ingredients

8 scrubbed Yukon Golden potatoes, halved lengthwise

4 tbsp olive oil

8 scrubbed red potatoes, halved lengthwise

4 peeled sweet potatoes, cut into wedges

8 carrots, halved lengthwise

4 red onions, cut into wedges

4 peeled parsnips, cut into wedges

4 red peeled beets, cut into wedges

4 tbsp thyme, chopped

1 tbsp ground cumin

2 tsp smoked paprika

1 garlic bulb, top cut off

Salt and ground black pepper to taste

Directions

Preheat your electric smoker to 275°F by adding apple wood chips. Preheat a cast-iron casserole by placing it on a smoking rack, then add 2 tbsp of olive oil. Place the red potatoes, potatoes, sweet potatoes, carrots, red onions, parsnips, beets, thyme, cumin, smoked paprika, garlic, salt, and pepper in a bowl. Drizzle with the remaining olive oil and toss to coat.

Pour the vegetables into the preheated casserole and smoke for 50-60 minutes, gently tossing occasionally until the vegetables are tender and caramelized.

Cinnamon Whiskey Glazed Pumpkin

Prep Time: 40 minutes | Cooking Time: 2-3 hours | Serves: 2

Ingredients

1 large pie pumpkin   Cooking spray

Seasoning ingredients

2 tbsp light brown sugar   ½ tsp ground ginger,
2 tsp ground cinnamon   ½ tsp orange zest, dried
½ tsp grated nutmeg   ¼ tsp ground allspice

Glaze ingredients

1 cup vegetable stock   2 tbsp cornstarch
¼ cup light brown sugar   4 oz cinnamon whiskey

Directions

To prepare the glaze, pour the vegetable stock into a small cooking pot over medium heat. Bring it to a boil and cook for 10 minutes. Then, add the brown sugar and stir to combine.

Mix the cornstarch and water together in a small bowl. Pour the slurry into the pot and cook for 2 minutes while stirring the liquid. Stir in the cinnamon whiskey for 1-2 minutes.

Mix the seasoning ingredients in a bowl. Wash and clean the pumpkin and cut it into slices with a knife. Take out the seeds and cut the slices into cubes. Transfer them to a baking tray. Spritz them with cooking spray and sprinkle with the seasoning mix. Brush with the previously prepared glaze and place in the smoker. Let it smoke for 2-3 hours at 225°F.

Smoked Bell Peppers & Zucchini

Prep Time: 40 minutes | Cooking Time: 2 hours | Serves: 2

Ingredients

4 zucchinis, cut into slices   4 tbsp olive oil
12 green onions   Sea salt and black pepper to taste
2 red bell peppers, sliced

Directions

Preheat the smoker to 225°F and add apple wood chips. Mix all the ingredients in a bowl. Transfer to a cast-iron skillet. Place in preheated smoker and smoke for 2 hours.

Pumpkin Bread Pudding

Prep Time: 40 minutes | Cook Time: 3 hours | Serves 8

Ingredients

1 lb bacon slices, chopped

6 eggs

2 cups heavy cream

3 tbsp thyme, chopped

Salt and ground black pepper to taste

1 (1-lb) pumpkin, cubed

3 leeks, thinly sliced

1 baguette loaf, diced

2 cups finely grated mozzarella cheese

8 pitted black olives

Directions

Preheat your electric smoker to 275°F by adding apple wood chips. Preheat a cast-iron baking pan by placing it on a smoking rack, then add the bacon. Smoke for 25-30 minutes, tossing occasionally. Remove the bacon to a plate. Add the pumpkin and leeks to the skillet and sprinkle with salt and pepper. Smoke for 30 minutes.

When the time is over, add the bread cubes to the skillet and gently stir to combine the ingredients. Beat the eggs with salt and pepper. Pour in the heavy cream and thyme and whisk again. Spoon the egg mixture evenly over the skillet ingredients.

Top with mozzarella cheese and black olives. Smoke for 50-60 minutes until golden brown, and a skewer comes out clean when inserted into the bread. Remove from the baking pan and let it cool on a wire rack. Serve sliced.

Pancetta & Brussels Sprout Sauté

Prep Time: 40 minutes | Cook Time: about 2 hours | Serves 8

Ingredients

2 tbsp olive oil

1 lb pancetta, cut into ½-inch pieces

4 shallots, trimmed and finely sliced

2 garlic cloves, minced

2 tbsp white wine

1 tsp fresh sage, chopped

2 lb Brussels sprouts, halved

Salt and ground black pepper to taste

Directions

Preheat your electric smoker to 275°F by adding apple wood chips. Preheat a cast-iron casserole by placing it on a smoking rack, then add the olive oil. Place the pancetta, shallots, and garlic into the casserole and smoke for 55-60 minutes, tossing occasionally.

Pour in the white wine, Brussels sprouts, sage, salt, and pepper and continue to smoke for 1 hour or until soft and golden. When ready, remove from the heat and leave to cool for a few minutes, then serve.

Buttered Black Beans

Prep Time: 40 minutes | Cook Time: about 2 hours | Serves 8

Ingredients

2 tbsp olive oil

1 yellow onion, diced

3 garlic cloves, minced

Salt and ground black pepper to taste

2 (14-oz) cans black beans

3 fresh bay leaves

½ tsp dried chili flakes

2 tsp smoked paprika

½ tsp ground cumin

3 cups vegetable stock

Directions

Preheat your electric smoker to 250°F by adding apple wood chips. Preheat a large cast-iron skillet by placing it on a smoking rack, then pour in the olive oil. Stir in the onion, garlic, salt, and pepper. Smoke for 25-30 minutes. Then, add the beans, bay leaves, chili flakes, smoked paprika, cumin and vegetable stock. Smoke for 60-90 minutes. Serve and enjoy!

Smoked Root Medley

Prep Time: 40 minutes | Cooking Time: 90 minutes | Serves: 4

Ingredients

2 russet potatoes, unpeeled and cut into chunks

4 large carrots cut into cubes

4 sweet potatoes, cut into chunks

½ cup olive oil

Salt and black pepper to taste

2 tbsp parsley, chopped

Directions

Preheat your smoker to 200°F by adding in the mild or any other wood chips. Toss all the vegetables with olive oil, salt, and pepper in a large bowl. Transfer them to a aluminum foil pan. Place the pan into the preheated smoker and cook for 60-80 minutes at 220°F.

Once the vegetables get tender, transfer to a serving plate and drizzle a bit more olive oil on top. Sprinkle with parsley and serve.

Spicy Stuffed Mushrooms Wrapped in Bacon

Prep Time: 40 minutes | Cooking Time: 90 minutes | Serves: 4

Ingredients

12 white mushrooms

12 bacon strips, sliced

1 tbsp olive oil

2 garlic cloves, chopped

Salt and black pepper to taste

1 jalapeño pepper, minced

½ cup hot sauce

Directions

Preheat your electric smoker to 225°F by adding apple wood chips and wait until smoke starts to come out. Remove the stems from the mushrooms and finely chop them. Transfer the chopped stems to a bowl. Add the garlic, jalapeño, salt, and pepper and toss to coat.

Drizzle the mushroom caps with olive oil and sprinkle them with salt and pepper. Spoon the jalapeño mixture into the mushroom caps. Wrap each mushroom with a bacon strip.

Twist the end of the bacon strips and let it drape down the sides of the mushrooms. Place these stuffed mushrooms filling side up onto a baking rack and smoke for 90 minutes. Serve with hot sauce.

Rosemary Potato Cake

Prep Time: 40 minutes | Cooking Time: 90 minutes | Serves: 6

Ingredients

6 potatoes, scrubbed but not skinned

3 tbsp olive oil

Salt and black pepper to taste

3 tbsp rosemary, chopped

Directions

Preheat the smoker to 220°F by adding wood chips of apple flavor. Sprayed a heavy skillet with oil and then set aside. Take a mandolin and thinly slice the potatoes. Place the potatoes in the skillet. As you add the slices, brush the potatoes with olive oil and sprinkle salt and pepper along with the rosemary.

Cook in the smoker until it starts to sizzle, about 1 hour. Carefully invert the torte on a flat plate. Return the torte to the cooking skillet and place it in the smoker for additional cooking for 30 minutes. Serve.

Garlicky Asparagus with Lemon

Prep Time: 40 minutes + marinating time | Cooking Time: 1.5 hours | Serves: 1

Ingredients

2 cups asparagus
Cooking spray
Salt and black pepper to taste

2 tbsp butter
2 garlic cloves, minced
1 lemon

Directions

Prepare the electric smoker for 2 hours at 200°F with mild or any other wood chips. Trim and cut the asparagus into a 1-inch length. Put the asparagus in hot boiling water for 1 minute and then drain the water. Pat dry the vegetables with a paper towel. Toss them with salt, pepper, and oil them with cooking spray.

Set the temperature of the smoker to 250°F and cooks the asparagus for 1.5 hours. Just before when the asparagus is ready to serve, melt the butter in a separate saucepan and add garlic. Do not fry the garlic.

Once the asparagus is cooked to its perfection, transfer it to the serving tray and then top it off with butter dressing. Cut the lemon in half and squeeze the juice over the top and serve.

Smoked Veggie Mix

Prep Time: 40 minutes | Cooking Time: 2 hours | Serves: 2

Ingredients

2 fresh corn ears, husks and silk strands removed
2 yellow squash, sliced
2 red onions, cubed
3 green bell peppers, cut into strips
1 yellow bell pepper, cut into strips

2 cups mushrooms, halved
2 tbsp cooking oil, vegetable
2 tbsp chicken seasoning

Directions

Preheat your electric smoker to 200°F with mild or any other wood chips. Cut the cor ears into pieces and place them in a large bowl. Add the remaining ingredients and toss to coat. Transfer them to the grill basket. Smoke for about 2 hours at 225°F. Once it's done, serve as a side dish.

Carrots & Potatoes with Balsamic Glaze

Prep Time: 40 minutes | Cooking Time: 2 hours | Serves: 3

Ingredients

1 lb sweet potatoes

½ lb Yukon gold potatoes

4 oz baby carrots

½ cup extra-virgin olive oil

Salt and pepper to taste

½ cup balsamic vinegar

Directions

Preheat your smoker to 225°F by adding mild or any other wood chips. Peel, wash, and cut all the potatoes into 2–inch chunks. Combine potato chunks with baby carrot.

Drizzle olive oil on the top. Season it with salt and pepper. Stir well to combine ingredients well. Place the ingredients in a large rack and smoke it for 1-2 hours. Once potatoes are tender, drizzle balsamic vinegar on top.

Tasty Smoked Paprika Cauliflower

Prep Time: 40 minutes | Cooking Time: 2 hours | Serves: 2

Ingredients

1 head cauliflower, cut into florets

3 tbsp olive oil

1 tbsp white pepper

2 tsp smoked paprika

Directions

Preheat your electric smoker to 250°F with mild or any other apple or cherry wood chips. Line a baking rack with the aluminum foil.

Take a large mixing bowl and combine olive oil, smoked paprika and white pepper, and cauliflower. Toss well. Smoke in electric smoke for 2 hours. Once it's done, serve.

Chipotle Smoked Corn with Cilantro

Prep Time: 40 minutes | Cooking Time: 2-3 hours | Serves: 8

Ingredients

8 corn ears

½ cup mayo

½ cup sour cream

1 handful of fresh cilantro, chopped

2 tsp paprika

1 tsp cumin

Black pepper to taste

3 oz spicy chipotle cream cheese

2 limes, sliced

Directions

Preheat your electric smoker to 225°F. Husk corn and remove the silk. Arrange the corn inside the smoker by tightly tying the husks together. Smoke for 2 hours. Combine the remaining ingredient in a small bowl. Serve it with smoked corn.

Thyme & Lemon Artichokes

Prep Time: 40 minutes + marinating time | Cooking Time: 2 hours | Serves: 2

Ingredients

2 artichokes

Dipping ingredients

½ cup melted butter

2 tsp dried thyme,

2 tbsp fresh lemon juice

Salt and black pepper to taste

Directions

Preheat your electric smoker to 200°F by adding mild or any other wood chips. Trim the spikes from the artichokes and cut the base. Steam the artichoke for 20 minutes, then rinse off and pat them dry. Smoke for 2 hours at 225°F. Mix the dipping ingredient in a bowl and then serve it with smoked artichokes.

Thyme Smoked Tomatoes

Prep Time: 40 minutes | Cooking Time: 60 minutes | Serves: 2

Ingredients

10 plum tomatoes

Salt and black pepper to taste

Thyme to taste

Directions

Preheat the smoker to 225°F by adding hickory smoker chips. Remember to soak the wood chips in water for 60 minutes before adding them to the smoker. Season the tomatoes with listed ingredients. Layer the tomatoes on a rack or baking pan, and then cook inside the smoker for 60 minutes. Serve as a side dish.

Onion Smoked Mushrooms

Prep Time: 40 minutes | Cooking Time: 45 minutes | Serves: 1

Ingredients

1 tbsp onion powder

1 tsp sugar

Salt and black pepper to taste

4 cups mushrooms

1 tbsp canola oil

Directions

Preheat the smoker to 350°F by adding apple wood chips. Combine mushroom along with the remaining ingredients in a bowl. Transfer the mushrooms to the smoking rack and place in your electric smoker. Cook for 30 minutes. Turn the temperature to 450°F and continue smoking for 15 more minutes. Serve.

Buttery Smoked Cabbage Side

Prep Time: 40 minutes | Cooking Time: 2 hours | Serves: 2

Ingredients

¼ cabbage head, sliced

3 tbsp Italian seasoning

1 stick butter

1 vegetable bouillon cube

Directions

Preheat the smoker, then add the hickory wood chips. Put the cabbage into a tinfoil pan and place the butter on top. Then sprinkle the crushed vegetable bouillon cube.

Sprinkle the Italian seasoning at the end. Wrap it in the tin foil, leaving the top slightly open. Once the smoke starts to build, place the tin foil pan into the smoker and cook it for 2 hours at 250°F. Once it's done, remove and serve.

Dijon Smoked Brussels Sprouts

Prep Time: 40 minutes | Cooking Time: 90 minutes | Serves: 2

Ingredients

1.5 lb Brussels sprouts

6 tbsp olive oil

2 tbsp Dijon mustard

6 cloves garlic, minced

2 sprig thyme

½ tsp smoked paprika

2 tsp apple cider vinegar

Salt and black pepper to taste

Directions

Preheat the electric smoker for two hours at 200°F by adding mild or wood chips. Chop the Brussels sprouts in a large bowl. Add in all the listed ingredients and toss well for fine coating. Place the Brussels sprouts in a non-stick rack and place them inside the smoker. Cook for 90 minutes at 220°F.

Flavorful Squash with Zucchini

Prep Time: 40 minutes + marinating time | Cooking Time: 1 hour | Serves: 3

Ingredients

4 tbsp balsamic vinegar

Salt and black pepper to taste

3 zucchinis

2 tbsp vegetable oil

1 butternut squash

Directions

Preheat your electric smoker for two hours at 200°F by adding mild or any other wood chips. Slice the vegetables into ½-inch halves. Brush the vegetable with oil and sprinkle salt and pepper on top. Smoke it for 60 minutes at 250°F. Once tender, take the vegetables out and drizzle vinegar on top.

Thyme Smoked Potatoes

Prep Time: 40 minutes + marinating time | Cooking Time: 2 hours | Serves: 2

Ingredients

⅓ cup olive oil

4 large potatoes

Salt and black pepper to taste

1 tbsp onion powder

1 tsp garlic powder

1 tsp dried thyme

Directions

Preheat the electric smoker for two hours at 200°F by adding mild or any other wood chips. Cut the potatoes in half and then brush with a generous amount of olive oil. Sprinkle salt, onion powder, garlic powder, dried thyme, and pepper on top. Smoke for 2 hours at 225°F.

Cheddar & Prosciutto Sandwiches

Prep Time: 50 minutes | Cooking Time: 45 minutes | Serves: 3

Ingredients

6 whole grain bread slices

2 tbsp butter, softened

6 cheddar cheese slices

1 onion

6 prosciutto slices

Directions

Preheat your electric smoker to 250°F. Place the onion in the smoker and let it cook for 45 minutes. Remove and then slice thinly. Smear butter on each bread slice.

Top three of the bread slices with one cheese slice of, a generous amount of onion, one slice of prosciutto and one slice of cheddar cheese. Place the remaining slices on the top of the cheddar cheese. Assemble all slices in the form of a sandwich. Serve and enjoy.

Balsamic Eggplants

Prep Time: 40 minutes + marinating time | Cooking Time: about 2 hours | Serves: 2

Ingredients

3 cloves garlic, minced

4 tbsp balsamic vinegar

Salt and black pepper to taste

4 eggplants

3 tbsp olive oil

Directions

Cut the eggplant into round, thick circles. Marinate the eggplant in a mixture of garlic, vinegar, salt, and pepper for 30 minutes.

Preheat your smoker to 250°F by adding apple-flavor wood chips. Transfer eggplant to the bowl and coat it with olive oil. Smoke in the electric smoker for 1 hour.

DESSERTS

Creamy Chocolate Tart

Prep Time: 50 Minutes | Cooking Time: 80 Minutes | Serves: 3

Ingredients

2 cups chocolate, chopped

Tart Topping

1.5 cups all-purpose flour

4 tbsp sugar

1 tsp baking powder

1 cup whipped cream for topping

5 tbsp cocoa powder

½ cup sour cream

Directions

Preheat your smoker to 250°F and add wood chips and wait until the smoke is established. In a medium bowl, mix the sugar, flour, baking soda, and cocoa powder. Add the sour cream. Mix gently to form a dough. Add chocolate pieces to a baking bowl.

Pour the dough mixture on top. Place it in the smoker and cook for 80 minutes or until the top gets brown and bubbling. Serve with whipped cream if desired.

Oat Crumble with Cherries & Raisins

Prep Time: 50 Minutes | Cooking Time: 3 Hours | Serves: 4

Ingredients

1 cup cherries, pitted

¾ cup dark brown sugar

1 cup self-rising flour

1.5 cup quick oats

⅓ cup all-purpose flour

½ cup raisins

⅓ cup butter

Directions

Place the cherries, brown sugar, and flour in a bowl and mix gently. Take the aluminum pan and coat it with oil spray. Spoon the flour filling into the aluminum pan.

Add oats, raisins, butter, and flour. Mix well until it is lumpy in consistency. Cook in an electric smoker for 3 hours at 260°F. Once it's done, serve.

Lemon Crumble with Blueberries

Prep Time: 40 Minutes | Cooking Time: 4 Hours | Serves: 4

Ingredients

1 cup blueberries

¾ cup dark brown sugar

½ cup self-rising flour

Crumble ingredients

1.5 cups quick-cooking oats

⅓ cup all-purpose flour

½ cup packed brown sugar

2 tsp lemon zest, grated

2 tbsp lemon juice

2 tsp cinnamon

⅓ cup butter

Directions

Place the washed blueberries in a mixing bowl and add sugar, lemon zest, lemon juice, and flour. Mix all the ingredients well. Take an aluminum pan and coat it with oil spray. Spoon the filling into the pan.

Then combine all the crumble ingredients in a separate bowl and pour over the blueberry mixture in the pan. Cook in the electric smoker for 4 hours at 260°F. Once done, serve.

Peach Baked Cobbler

Prep Time: 50 Minutes | Cooking Time: 3 Hours | Serves: 4

Ingredients

2 tsp melted butter

3 lb sliced peaches

½ cup maple syrup

1 cup self-rising flour

3/4 tsp baking powder

1 pinch cinnamon

1 pinch salt

⅓ cup unsalted butter, cut into small cubes

⅓ cup white sugar

2 eggs

½ tsp vanilla

Directions

Set the electric smoker temperature to 220°F and add cherry wood chips. Coat a large heatproof pan with melted butter. Take a bowl and toss peaches with maple syrup.

In a small bowl, combine flour, baking powder, salt and cinnamon, and set it aside.

In a separate bowl, mix butter along with sugar. Then add eggs and the vanilla extract.

Combine the flour mixture with the egg mixture. Spoon this batter on top of peaches. Cook in the electric smoker for 3 hours at 260°F. Once done, serve.

Vanilla Rhubarb Cake

Prep Time: 40 minutes | Cooking Time: 3 Hours | Serves: 3

Ingredients

1 lb rhubarb, chopped
⅓ cup brown sugar
Pinch of salt

1 tsp lemon juice
1 tbsp lemon zest
2 tsp vanilla extract

Cobbler Topping

1.5 cups all-purpose flour
4 tbsp sugar
1 tsp baking powder

¼ tsp kosher salt
10 tbsp unsalted butter
⅓ cup sour cream

Directions

Start your electric smoker and add mild flavor wood chips and wait until the smoke is established. Set temperature to 260°F. Take a medium bowl and mix cobbler topping, ingredients including salt, flour, baking powder, and sugar. Add butter and sour cream.

Mix gently with the fork to form the smooth dough. Take a small bowl and then mix chopped rhubarb, lemon juice, lemon zest, vanilla extract, salt, and sugar.

Transfer the mixture to the desired baking dish. Spoon the prepared dough on top. Smoke for 3 hours or until the top gets brown and bubbling. Serve.

RUBS AND SEASONINGS

Chili Rub

Prep Time: 40 minutes | Cooking Time: 60 -120 minutes | Serves: 3

Ingredients

½ cup cane sugar

⅓ cup chili powder

2 tbsp granulated onion

2 tbsp granulated garlic

1 tbsp dried chilies

1 tbsp dill weed

3 tbsp lemon powder

2 tbsp cumin, ground

2 tbsp celery seeds

2 tbsp basil

½ tbsp dried rosemary

½ tbsp mustard powder

Directions

Preheat your electric smoker to 220°F. Combine all the spices in a bowl. Use a cold smoker attachment and fire up the apple wood chips until the temperature reaches 100°F.

Next, pour the spice mix into an aluminum pie pan. Place the pan inside the smoker and let it smoke for 1 or 2 hours. After an hour, the spices should be smoked to perfection. Store it in a tight jar for future use.

Sweet Mustard Rub

Prep Time: 40 minutes | Cooking Time: 120 minutes | Serves: 3

Ingredients

½ cup paprika

½ tsp brown sugar

2 tbsp salt

4 tbsp white pepper

4 tbsp mustard

Directions

Combine all the spices in a bowl. Preheat your electric smoker to 220°F. Use a cold smoker attachment and fire up the apple wood chips until the temperature reaches 100°F.

Pour the spice mix into an aluminum pie pan. Place the pan inside the smoker and smoke for 2 hours. Store it in a tight jar.

Peppered Spice Rub

Prep Time: 40 minutes | Cooking Time: 2 hours | Serves: 4

Ingredients

4 tbsp black pepper

4 tbsp white pepper

1 tbsp red pepper

2 tbsp onion powder

2 tsp garlic powder

1 tbsp dried thyme

2 tbsp paprika

4 tbsp dried oregano

Directions

Combine all the spices in a bowl. Preheat your electric smoker to 220°F. Use a cold smoker attachment and fire up the hickory wood chips until the temperature reaches 100°F.

Take an aluminum pan and place spices into it. Place in the smoker and smoke for 2 hours. Store it in a tight jar.

Herby Chicken Rub

Prep Time: 40 minutes | Cooking Time: 1-2 hours | Serves: 2

Ingredients

1 tsp sea salt

4 tsp dried basil

4 tsp crushed dried rosemary

2 tsp garlic powder

4 tsp dry mustard powder

1 tsp paprika

¼ tsp ground black pepper

¼ tsp ground dried thyme

½ tsp celery seed

1 tsp dried parsley

½ tsp ground cumin

½ tsp cayenne pepper

Directions

Combine all the spices in a large bowl. Preheat your electric smoker to 220°F. Use a cold smoker attachment and fire up the apple wood chips until the temperature reaches 100°F.

Pour the spice mix into an aluminum pie pan. Place inside the smoker and close the door. After 2 hours, the spices should be smoked to perfection. Store it in a tight jar for future use.

Facile Jerky Seasoning

Prep Time: 40 minutes | Cooking Time: 2 hours | Serves: 1

Ingredients

6 tbsp dried minced onion

4 tsp dried thyme

2 tsp ground allspice powder

1 tsp ground black pepper

2 tsp ground cinnamon

2 tsp cayenne pepper

Directions

Preheat your electric smoker to 220°F. Combine all the spices in a bowl. Use a cold smoker attachment and fire up the apple-flavored wood chips until the temperature reaches 100°F.

Next, pour the spice mix into an aluminum pie pan. Place the pan inside the smoker and let it smoke for 2 hours. Store spices in a tight jar for future use.

Spicy BBQ Rub

Prep Time: 40 minutes | Cooking Time: 60-120 minutes | Serves: 2

Ingredients

½ cup brown sugar

½ cup paprika

1 tbsp ground black pepper

½ tbsp salt

3 tbsp chili powder

4 tbsp garlic powder

4 tbsp onion powder

1 tsp cayenne pepper

Directions

Combine all the spices in a bowl. Preheat your electric smoker to 220°F. Use a cold smoker attachment and fire up the apple wood chips until the temperature reaches 100°F.

Next, take an aluminum pie pan and place the spices from the bowl into it. Place the pan inside the smoker and let it smoke for 1 to 2 hours. Store it in a tight jar for future use.

Homemade Cajun Spice

Prep Time: 40 minutes | Cooking Time: 60 minutes | Serves: 4

Ingredients

½ tbsp salt

4 tsp ground cayenne pepper

3 tsp ground white pepper

4 tsp ground black pepper

4 tsp paprika

4 tsp onion powder

3 tsp garlic powder

Directions

Preheat your electric smoker to 220°F. Combine all the spices in a bowl. Use a cold smoker attachment and fire up the apple wood chips until the temperature reaches 100°F.

Next, pour the spice mix into an aluminum pie pan. Place the pan inside the smoker and let it smoke for one hour. After an hour, the spices should be smoked to perfection. Store spices in a tight jar for future use.

Citrus Seafood Seasoning

Prep Time: 40 minutes | Cooking Time: 120 minutes | Serves: 4

Ingredients

2 tsp paprika

4 tsp cinnamon

3 tsp ground ginger

2 tsp ground cumin

2 tsp ground coriander

2 tsp dried lemon peel

4 tsp onion powder

2 tsp lemon pepper

2 tsp dried parsley

2 tsp dried cilantro

2 tsp garlic powder

Directions

Preheat your electric smoker to 220°F. Combine all the spices in a bowl. Use a cold smoker attachment and fire up with the cherry wood chips until the temperature reaches 100°F.

Next, pour the spice mix into an aluminum pie pan. Place the pan inside the smoker and let it smoke for 2 hours. After 2 hours, the spices should be smoked to perfection. Store in the tight jar for future use.

Traditional Rub

Prep Time: 40 minutes | Cooking Time: 2 hours | Serves: 1

Ingredients

4 tbsp brown sugar

1 tbsp paprika

2 tbsp salt

1 tbsp ground black pepper

2 tsp garlic powder

Directions

Preheat your electric smoker to 220°F. Combine all the spices in a bowl. Use a cold smoker attachment and fire up the mildly flavored wood chips until the temperature reaches 100°F.

Next, pour the spice mix into an aluminum pie pan. Place the pan inside the smoker and let it smoke for 2 hours. After 2 hours, the spices should be smoked to perfection. Store it in a tight jar for future use.

Easy Smoked Salt

Prep Time: 40 minutes | Cooking Time: 60 minutes | Serves: 2

Ingredients

½ cup kosher salt

Directions

Preheat your electric smoker to 220°F. Use a cold smoker attachment and fire up the apple wood chips until the temperature reaches 100°F.

Next, take an aluminum pie pan and place about ½ cup of kosher salt into it. Place in the smoker to start the smoking process. After 1 hour, the salt should be smoked to its perfection. Store it in a tight jar for future use.

Made in the USA
Monee, IL
14 June 2023

35780866R00068